A Sunset Book

Fresh-Water Fishing Illustrated

HOW TO CATCH FISH IN THE WEST

Text and Illustrations by
Morie Morrison

LANE BOOKS • MENLO PARK, CALIF.

Preface

Fresh-water fishing from the Rockies west is not exactly like it is in other parts of the world, and nobody understands the differences better than Morie Morrison.

The author has fished the headwaters of the Euphrates River in Turkey, has angled in many streams of western Europe, has wet lines in great fishing holes around these United States, and has tried his hand in the waters of some Pacific islands. He even took up skin diving at one point, so he could get a better look at how fish behave.

He has written about fishing (and other sports) as a newspaperman, syndicated columnist, and as the author of five other how-to-do-it books.

But the main thing is, he has caught a tremendous number of fish, and he can explain in clear language how he did it. Without unnecessary first-person recitals of how it was at 4 o'clock one morning on the south fork of the "you-name-it" when he was the first man to fish there since the Indians, Morie Morrison presents information which the reader will need when *he* tries those waters.

The key of explaining the unique approach of this book is this: Know the adversary—learn to think like a fish. Morie Morrison's text and drawings work together to explain how fish live in Western lakes and streams, and how an angler can catch them unawares, with a hook.

The Editors
Sunset Books

Seventh Printing May 1972

CONTENTS

Cover photograph by Martin Litton

Western Fishing Country

As an airplane flies west over the summit of the Rocky Mountains its occupants can gaze at countless lakes, rivers, and small creeks in the land below.

Some streams are seen as tiny slivers of silver. Often they disappear as they wind through canyons and primitive forests, to reappear as meandering ribbons tracing their ways through meadows, valleys, and waste lands. Others seem to hide forever as they enter a clump of green or a deep gorge.

Occasionally a river takes a rest in a blue lake before continuing its journey. White threads of water meet to form larger streams; orchards and farm lands come into view as if to give notice that the soil and water are good.

Patchworks of farms surround cities; roads and highways crisscross the countryside, and industries blow smoke. But through it all, the streams keep flowing, with accompanying lakes looking like scattered bits of confetti.

Everything seems to be in such good order that an air traveler invariably wishes he lived in that land he sees.

Soon the streams lead into larger bodies of water. They form dammed lakes to add water reserves to the growing west. Unless a map is a recent one, these bodies of water are not shown in the mapmaker's blue ink because they are so new.

Out of these reservoirs pour bigger streams. And in practically no time at all the air traveler sees them emptying into bays and finally the Pacific Ocean.

As the pilot or passenger gazes at this beautiful landscape he frequently thinks or dreams himself down to earth. His thoughts draw mental pictures about clear, cool waters making bubbly music as they flow through miles of shaded banks bordered by beautiful azaleas, or rhododendrons, or tree ferns. He dreams about crystal clear lakes sitting in the laps of granite mountains or of the laughter he imagines must come from large waters dotted with pleasure boats.

He thinks about scrub willows along a river's edge and how the current sometimes makes the branches bow back and forth as if to say hello. He hears a fluttering bird, sees a big trout make dimples on the quiet surface of a pool, marvels at the natural cleanness of granite rocks which prehistoric glaciers exposed, smells the pine and fir.

He feels the silence of the forests and thinks about the tall, western trees that always seem to be pushing their tops straight up toward heaven and God. Honesty and purpose is what they imply as they rise from their carpets of loveliness.

He thinks about the beauty of the mountains and how nature has a way of keeping many western forests devoid of tangling undergrowth, and looking instead like well-manicured parks.

To fishermen and travelers this is big country. It is formed by several of the world's largest mountain ranges: The Rockies, Sierras, and Cascades—geologic giants creating a land mass of peaks and valleys from Canada to Mexico.

From the air, their ramparts are seen to form a country of tumbled mountains and serrated peaks rising to 14,000 feet and more. The sides are steep where they form protective walls for the long valleys at their feet—valleys of rugged wilderness, rich tablelands, and peaceful lands reflecting farm prosperity.

The west sides of the ranges are green because that is where the prevailing winds and storms from the Pacific Ocean drop most of their water. These west slopes have a greater number of fine fishing streams and lakes.

The east sides are drier, but modern water conservation and irrigation methods are beginning to turn the arid eastern lowlands into a green area, too.

This awesomely beautiful western land with its contrasting formations and climates is challenging country to a fisherman. Every kind of lake or steam is there—cold or warm, clear or murky, high or low, rich or poor, big or little, accessible or inaccessible.

In these waters are the aristocrats of gamefish. Rainbow, golden, cutthroat, brown, lake, brook, and Dolly Varden trout; steelhead, king, and silver salmon; and largemouth and smallmouth bass. With them are less famous but equally edible fish: bluegill, perch, crappie, catfish, sturgeon, striped bass, and many more.

No other wild creature is studied by so many Westerners as is the trout. Since the traditional place to seek trout has been in streams and rivers, these waters have received the largest share of anglers' attention. Greater numbers of fishermen and greater numbers of artificial lakes have made still waters increasingly popular.

This, then, is the picture of western fishing country as a high-flying pilot might see it. It is a vast area where much of the land is still new and filled with natural beauty a true sportsman loves. A place to relax and think things over—quietly.

It is no wonder that after a few days on a stream or lake, a man frequently returns to his home and job with a feeling of spiritual gain. The beauty of nature is almost certain to make him feel that way.

But now, amid its beauty, a major problem has come to the west. Population numbers have exploded into fantastic figures in the past decade. Millions of newcomers have moved west permanently. Millions of tourists join them as temporary residents. This has made the west a land of "mores."

More people need more housing. More automobiles need more highways. More roofs need more TV antennae. More fishermen need more fish.

These conditions have created pressures on the entire political and administrative system, and fishing pressures are no exception. In every western state authorities are being constantly reminded that something should be done about stocking and growing more fish to improve fishing.

Sometimes fishermen themselves carelessly undo the work of fish management. At other times industry harms fish populations. And, at still other times, the fish management people are not able to do an ideal job. Whatever the case may be, it is no time to lay blame about.

For the long-term good of fish and fishermen it is a time to cooperate, and to remember that despite depredation, over-population, and acts harmful to fish populations, western waters contain an abundance of gamefish that are waiting right now for a knowing angler to challenge them.

About Fish and Fishermen

Fresh-water gamefish, particularly trout, are an old-fashioned form of animal life. Anatomically, they have not moved up the evolutionary ladder of fishdom for many millions of years. In fact, they are rather closely related to fishes dating as far back as 400,000,000 B.C.

This puts the trout and salmon family (along with two favorite buddies, the angleworm and caddis fly) in action 200,000,000 years ahead of dinosaurs and flying reptiles. About 30 million years ago the trout became firmly established as a specific species, and despite geologic change, wars, pestilence, airplanes, and television, trout have remained much the same.

The bass, humble catfish, and despised carp have done a little better. Somewhere along the line they developed appendages and organs which scientists point to as advancements in fish evolution, and so they are ahead of trout. Not much. But a little.

An interesting thing about these fish is that they have lived all this time without giving it a thought, because their brainpower hasn't improved any more than the rest of them. Consequently, they act almost entirely on impulse instead of reason. This is why scientists call the fish a reflex animal. His instinct and body muscles govern his actions much more than his brain does. His greatest instinct, or reflex, is toward survival and away from possible danger.

Therefore, to catch a fish an angler will have his best luck when he works on some survival reflex, such as a fish's almost constant desire to eat something. In almost all cases an angler's main job is to present his bait at a place where fish lie and in a way that will cause the fish to take it instead of arousing his sense of danger.

This, in a nutshell, is why a youngster sometimes catches fish with a hook made from a bent pin while an expensively equipped angler fishing nearby gets skunked. The boy tempts the fish and the man scares him.

WHY FISH ACT THAT WAY

Reflex actions are triggered by the stimulation of taste, sight, hearing, feel, and other physiological senses. Some of these stimuli-reflex actions cause a fish to behave the way he does. These are important points for a fisherman to know. Very important. Not only do they give him a better understanding of fishing, they also give a man who has failed to catch anything some excellent information he can use to produce convincing alibis. These facts enable him to stand before friends and with a ring of knowing authority lecture about fish, fishing conditions, and why the fish didn't bite.

Often, as people listen to a lecture of this kind, they turn to each other and whisper, "This guy really knows what he's talking about. He's a terrific fisherman, isn't he?" A man with an empty creel cannot ask for a higher compliment than that.

Therefore, in the primary interests of fish lore and with some secondary dividends in the alibi department, the following information about the physiology of fish is offered.

The senses of fish...and how to fool them

A gamefish is extremely suspicious. What he sees or feels triggers instinctive desires toward self-preservation.

The outer "skin" of a gamefish is alive. It gives his entire body a delicate sense of touch.

In general, a human being has no more organs than a fish. Each has eyes to see food or danger, muscles to create movement, a skeleton on which the muscles work, a stomach to digest food, circulating blood, a disposal system to get rid of waste products, a brain, lungs, and so forth. The main difference between a fish and a man, therefore, is not how many organs are present, but how well the brain and body can use them, and how well the senses have been developed.

The brain: The fish's brain is smaller and less developed than those of many animals. The fish has no thought center for figuring things out, and his actions are, to a great extent, dominated by what he sees.

A fish's brain does not store information for future use. His memory is a short one. If severely frightened by a noise, or even a hook, he will forget about the incident within 15 minutes. A big grand-pappy trout owes his longevity to being careful instead of being smart.

Taste: Fish show a wide range of tastes—from catfish, which devour odorous, decayed bait with relish, to native trout, which may go so far as to refuse a bruised but still tasty worm.

To illustrate that fish do have taste, those caught with real food will often have the hook lodged inside the mouth, or down the throat if they have had any chance to swallow the food. On the other hand, when fish are caught on artificial lures the hook is generally found in the lip. It is almost never swallowed.

One reason is taste. With bait, the fish tasted, swallowed, and got hooked in the mouth or throat.

With an artificial lure, the fish tasted it, or hit it, tried to spit it out, and got hooked in or near the lip. (Granted, lures are often presented in a way that makes them more difficult to swallow, but then the fish is seldom interested in a still lure—it usually has to be in motion to attract his attention.)

The appetites of fish vary, and it is the job of a fisherman to find out what they will or will not eat at any one moment. In a river, trout may refuse worms while in a tributary stream they may take wrigglers ravenously. Then, without warning, the situation may reverse, causing conditions hard for any fisherman to understand or predict.

Touch: The fish gets his sense of touch through an outer "skin," which is alive. Composed of living cells in the form of mucous or slime, this semi-liquid medium surrounds the fish on all sides and is what makes him so slippery. Because the outer layer is alive, the fish has a delicate sense of touch. But since whatever touches the fish is felt widely throughout the body, and there is no highly developed brain to evaluate what has been touched and why, the fish's reaction to touch is generally one of fear. Higher animal forms which have a covering of dry skin—and in most cases fur on top of that—to protect their nerve-endings are usually more curious than afraid.

The layer of slime on a fish's body also serves several purposes besides touch. It acts as a lubricant to permit the fish's body to slide through water with minimum friction, to increase speed and conserve energy. It is a protection against disease, such as fun-

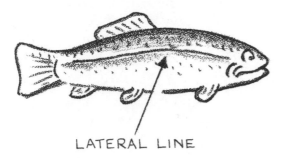

LATERAL LINE

The lateral line, which stretches from gills to tail, provides keen sensitivity to low-frequency sound vibrations.

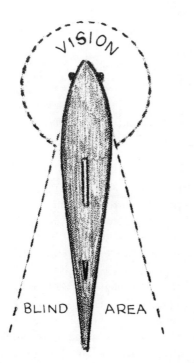

VISION

BLIND AREA

Below the surface, a fish can see much better than a man because his eyes protrude from the sides of his head.

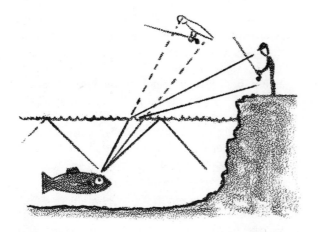

When a fish gazes up through the water's surface, he gets a distorted look at things because of light refraction.

gus, or against attack by parasites. It helps make the fish water-tight and allows his oxygen manufacturing equipment to work more efficiently.

Hearing: Fish can hear. They have no external or middle ear, but they do have an inner ear which is well developed. It operates in much the same manner as the human ear.

Sound vibrations are also detected by a special network of cells lying on a lateral line on each side of the fish. This is a narrow streak, usually a black line. It provides keen sensitivity to low frequency vibrations such as those caused by a man walking on wet gravel. Some people call this a fish's sixth sense.

Fish are most sensitive to sound vibrations created in or transmitted through water, such as crunching footsteps on damp ground, noisy oarlocks, or big feet on the stream bottom. Goldfish (carp) have the best hearing and can pick up the vibrations of human voices rather well. It is not unusual to see a goldfish in a bowl swim to the surface when his master calls because he recognizes the voice and has learned to associate it with feeding time. Trout and bass, however, cannot pick up the tone range of human voices. So when fishermen talk to each other, they can feel assured the fish are not paying any attention.

Sight: Trout and bass have a horizontal, below-the-surface vision of 300°, almost a complete circle. The blind spot is a 60° area behind the tail. If a stream fisherman wants to reduce the chances of being seen, he should approach fish from the rear as they face into the current.

The above-water vision of a fish is far more limited. Because the surface serves as a kind of mirror, a fish can see only in a cone of about 90°. What he sees in that cone is distorted by refraction at the surface. Therefore, the way for a fisherman to approach the clear waters of a lake or stream without being seen by the fish is to stay low and sneak up from behind if possible. To approach shallow waters, it may be necessary to crawl or creep on the stomach to keep out of sight.

Color perception: Fish seem to distinguish between the primary colors, but their ability to determine secondary and other in-between tones, such as green, purple, or tan, seems to depend upon the species.

All colors are affected by clarity of the water, amount of sunlight, and depth of water. In slightly muddy water, for example, what appears as bright yellow on the surface may appear to be orange at a 5-foot depth, and red at a 10-foot depth because of these factors. In crystal clear water the bright yellow won't begin to appear orange until a 20-foot depth is reached. Therefore water clarity (which affects the amount and depth of sunlight penetration) is as important to consider as a lure's color.

It is accepted that red is the most exciting color. An interesting bit of evidence about a fish's reaction to red came to light a few years ago when California Fish and Game Department biologists attached colored tags to the ventral fins of trout at their Mount Shasta hatchery, to study fish behavior during scheduled tests. Trout wearing red tags were continually attacked by other fish, while fish wearing green, yellow, blue, and white tags swam unmolested. Once the red tags were discarded, the tests proceeded normally.

The backbone: Higher forms of animal life can use separate muscles. For example, a dog can lift a leg to scratch its head, or a man can reach for a pencil to sign a credit card in a gasoline station. But when a fish was designed many millions of years ago, there was no apparent need for separate muscular development, and the fish hasn't seen fit to change with the times.

The fish has a body wall of muscles covering its backbone. When he moves, the entire body takes part in the movement from head to tail. It is all or nothing at all.

Fins: The fins on a fish are his limbs. The middle fins are the dorsal, caudal, and anal. The paired fins are the pectoral, behind the head, and the pelvic, on the lower part of the body. The dorsal and anal fins act as keels; the paired fins are rudders, and the caudal fin (tail) helps create power for swimming.

Blood: Fish have red blood, like man's, but it is not in the same proportion to body weight. Whereas a human being's blood runs 6% or more of his body weight, the amount in a fish is much smaller and ranges from 1.5% to 2.5%.

This is an extremely important fact for a fisherman to know and understand, because it has a great part in the playing and landing of a hooked fish. This is why: A primary function of blood is to transport oxygen in the form of blood sugar. As the body exercises, it burns the blood sugar to get oxygen so as to create muscular energy. As the oxygen is reduced, energy is reduced.

A large fish can often be caught on light tackle because as he fights the hook, oxygen is burned away quickly. Suddenly the point is reached where almost all of the fish's energy disappears and he will start floating belly-up, forced to give up the battle. Skilled fishermen know about this energy weakness and keep a controlled line to play fish aggressively so as to help create fatigue in the fish as soon as possible.

Blood pressure: Fish have low blood pressure. This

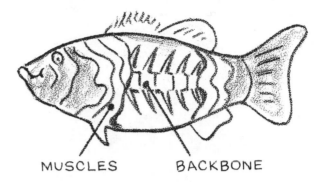

The fish has a backbone and thus is a vertebrate. This places him high among the water-borne forms of life.

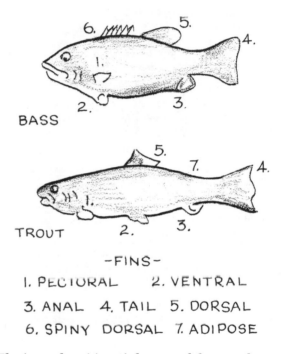

BASS

TROUT

-FINS-
1. PECTORAL   2. VENTRAL
3. ANAL   4. TAIL   5. DORSAL
6. SPINY DORSAL   7. ADIPOSE

The forward position of the ventral fins on a bass are a sign of greater evolutionary advancement than the trout.

Fish have low blood pressure. They are not bothered with heart trouble, but they become exhausted easily.

When black bass get ready to spawn, it is the male who builds the nest. Then he attracts a female.

With trout, the female is the nest maker. After she scoops a trough in gravel, she attracts a male to it.

affects their behavior, because a fish's body temperature is generally about the same as the surrounding water. Any abrupt change from warm or cold is noticed by a fish immediately. This is one of the main reasons lake fish change their swimming depths, and is discussed in detail in the chapter about water temperatures.

Swim bladder: Fish have a bladder filled with nitrogen to help provide flotability.

Believers in the barometric pressure theory of fish feeding maintain that when atmospheric pressure suddenly rises or falls, the water compression changes. They contend that a fish is sensitive to such pressure changes because they cause the gas in the fish's bladder to expand or contract so as to accommodate itself to the change in water pressure.

Because a change of pressure is uncomfortable to a fish, it may swim restlessly, but will not feed, according to the theory. It takes about three hours for the fish to adjust to the new situation.

The fishermen who support this theory claim that sudden weather changes are the reason fish sometimes won't eat before a rainstorm, and at other times will gobble anything. It depends upon whether the rain represents a pressure front just coming in, or one that has prevailed for some time.

Sex: Sex behavior varies with the species.

Bass depend upon the male to build a nest in the shallows of a lake. After a male completes his nest he blows a few bubbles to attract a female. She swims by, lays her eggs and departs, leaving the male to cover them with milt and then with protective mud. After that, he guards the nest until the eggs hatch.

During this time he will hit any suspicious article that drifts by the nest, and this is why spawning areas are sometimes closed to fishermen during the hatching season. The male defender can be caught too easily.

With trout, the female is the nest maker. The female uses her tail to scoop a trough in the gravel bottom of the stream, and as she gets ready to lay her eggs a male swims beside her, prepared to squirt sperm milk over the roe exactly as it is released. The female then sweeps gravel over the fertilized eggs.

This teamwork is necessary because the eggs are laid and fertilized in current. Unless the job is done with split-second timing, the entire operation will float downstream and be a failure.

HOME IN THE WATERY RANGE

If a stream fish, especially a brown or brook trout, finds a good hole with the kind of bubbling water that ventilates his home with needed oxygen and flows in a favorable, food-filled current, he may settle down there for a good part of his life. Some rainbows are like this, while others prefer to move around in a stream. Migratory fish such as salmon or steelhead have the urge to travel long distances and never do settle down in one place.

Lake fish have to lead a nomadic life, since there is no dependable current to bring food to them.

A stream fish cannot live in an attractive hole without an occasional battle. Other fish are certain to be envious of the spot and periodically there is an underwater fight for control of it. This is one of the reasons a choice fishing hole often produces more than one big fish. If the chief resident is hooked and leaves the place for a frying pan, it doesn't take long for another big one to notice the vacancy and move in. And because a fish's memory is short and his logic poor, within a half hour the new resident is ready to do business in the same hole and he may hit the same kind of well-presented lure that took away the former owner.

FISH ARE USUALLY HUNGRY

From birth to death the main mission in life of a fish seems to be satisfying his hunger. Unless the water becomes polluted, is too cold or too warm for comfort, or he is frightened, a fish never seems to get enough to eat.

Sometimes he becomes a loner and seeks dark refuge beneath an undercut bank or in a tangle of logs. These spots are popular because he can lie fearlessly and hungrily in a shadowy eddy that keeps flotsam whirling before his finicky eye.

In such a protected place he can take his time to make careful selection of what he eats, and at times he can become very fussy, which disappointed anglers often find out. For example, at 10 A.M. a trout may crave worms, and at 11 A.M. he won't look at a worm but will wait for drowned ants instead. This sudden change in feeding can drive an angler to distraction.

But for a gamefish it is the cautious and best way to grow to a big old-timer, which fishermen love to call a "grandpappy" or "submarine."

FISHING BY THE CLOCK

Freshwater fish are often hungriest at breakfast time. Unless there is a bright moon at night, they seem to fast during darkness. For a trout or black bass, the main business of which is eating, this is a long time.

The dawn hours produce fine fishing in most cases (except high lakes where the water doesn't warm up enough until noon). However, for the average fisherman, late afternoon and early evening are the best fishing hours because they are more convenient and because this is also a time of active feeding.

Because he knows the horrors of an empty stomach at midnight, a fish intuitively fills his stomach at dusk. At this time every fish in a lake or stream becomes selfish, eager, and less careful of what he swallows. The eagerness to eat builds a high degree of competitiveness; selfishness rather than fear controls a fish's actions. Big ones come out of the shadows and deep water to cruise the shallows in search of food, without the daylight fears of bright light, strange shadows, and marauders such as snakes, turtles, birds, animals, and even people.

Gamefish feel safe in protected places, such as beneath an undercut bank in a stream.

Fish do not like bright daylight. They prefer to visit shallow waters when the sun is low in the sky.

Of all the factors that might affect a fish's appetite, water temperature seems to be one of the most important.

Freshwater gamefish are divided into two main camps—coldwater and warmwater fish. Trout and salmon are called coldwater fish because they are found chiefly in the relatively cold waters of mountain areas and coastal streams. The group known as warmwater fish includes black bass, sunfish, and catfish, and its members are found chiefly in the warmer waters of the lowlands.

TROUT FEEDING HABITS

Trout do not like water colder than 40°, even though they can exist at lower temperatures. They also dislike water that warms to 70° and more. When temperatures rise above their liking, trout look for bubbly, aerated water in cool holes. They lie quietly all day, and feed at night when it is cooler.

The favorite temperature range for native trout in natural conditions is in the 52-60° bracket. This is about where an angler can feel the chill of the water through his rubber boots but not be uncomfortable about it.

Planted trout, used to the stepped-up conditions of modern hatcheries, enjoy a warmer temperature than the natives. Planted fish favor a 57-65° range for frisky activity.

The following paragraphs give a general picture of trout feeding habits. For a fuller discussion see the section "Limnology" starting on page 45.

In general, the fisherman should understand that trout in waters of 50° or less digest food slowly. Because they are less hungry they are less liable to take a lure or bait than they are in waters in the range from the upper 50's to the lower 60's. You may face the old truism, "When they ain't bitin' you ain't catchin'."

Also, in cold water there are few insect hatches. Therefore fly fishing, either wet or dry, will be slow. At such times it is best to use bait, or possibly spinners or wobblers.

In cold water the bait hooks should be small, the leaders fine, and sinkers as small as practicable. Trout appetites are finicky when it's cold. They will refuse anything that looks suspicious.

Trout begin taking underwater wet flies between 50 and 55°, especially along the bottom. But since trout instinctively know that nature does not begin producing fly hatches until temperatures reads 55° or more, they eat carefully.

Trout prefer cool waters. When water warms to 65° or more, they wish it would rain or snow to cool them off.

Favorite water temperature for dry fly action is in the 55-65° bracket because favorable weather will have warmed the waters to such an extent that insect hatching will be accelerated considerably. At this time mature insects begin rising to the surface and trout instinctively rise to swallow choice morsels on the top side.

Above 65°, trout fishing begins to taper off rapidly. Waters become too warm for comfort, and, as is the case with humans, "the heat just doesn't make a fellow feel like eating."

BASS FEEDING HABITS

King of the warmwater fish group is the largemouth black bass. Also known as "old bronzeback," he feels best at 70°.

A pretender to his throne is a cousin, the smallmouth black bass. This fellow prefers the lower warm temperatures of largemouth bass and the upper cool temperatures of trout waters. He is a real in-betweener.

The rest of the warmwater gamefish kingdom is composed largely of sunfish (such as bluegill and crappie), perch, catfish, and a few others which like their surroundings tepid.

Although largemouth bass are primarily a warmwater fish, they are hardy enough to do well in cold waters. Where they have been planted in the northern waters of such states as Washington and Montana

...affect feeding habits

WHERE IS MY HEATING PAD?

Bass enjoy life most in warm water. Water cooler than 60° makes them wish they had heating pads.

they have thrived. Admittedly, they have not grown so fast as their Arizona cousins because the northern waters get too cold for them to be year-around eaters; still the big fellows get along rather well almost anywhere and are a highly regarded gamefish throughout the country.

As with trout, the eating habits of a bass are largely governed by the temperature of the water which surrounds him. As with all fish, which are cold-blooded, he responds throughout his body to the water's coolness or warmth, which affects his metabolism to make him feel good, sometimes lazy, or even downright rotten.

50°: When waters are a cold 50° the largemouth doesn't eat much. During such conditions most bass fishermen will find things more enjoyable at home, where they can keep warm.

Although the angler may hook into an occasional smallmouth or pike in 50° water, he should never expect to tie into a largemouth because they are dormant. If one bites, he is a non-conformist or crazy or the victim of an expert in cold water fishing techniques.

55-60°: As water temperatures rise to 55°, largemouth begin to liven up. At 60° they feel good enough to become playful. At this point, they remember they are hungry after a long winter's nap, and can be encouraged to take lures, even in bright sunshine. Although they don't eat voraciously, they bite enough to provide good action.

60-65°: As the water warms to 65° largemouths begin to get ravenous. They will visit waters from one to four feet deep near rushes, logs, brush, and overhanging trees. These are favorite places because they can find seclusion in the shallows while enjoying the surface water's warmth.

In this situation the fisherman should use light tackle and make casts into shallow, warm water where there is protective cover for a bass to lie in what he feels is comfortable safety.

65-70°: This is a good temperature bracket. Largemouths range widely in this kind of water and feed often. During daytime they can be found beside rushes, underwater logs, or brush cover, beneath protective trees, and in the always-popular weed beds and lily pads

In early morning or at night they often visit the shoreline and feed in water as shallow as one foot. Surface lures, such as bass bugs in dark colors, are good choices for fishing these areas. It is important for the fisherman to keep from being seen because gamefish in shallow water are easily frightened.

70-75°: This is the temperature in which largemouth are at their active-eating best. During the day they prowl around all parts of their lake. In the evening they visit the shore at two to eight-foot depths. At this latter time they are a prime prospect for any type of surface lure. During the day they are best fished for with sub-surface lures.

75-80°: As water temperatures rise above 75°, largemouth begin looking for cool spots. During the day they lie 15 to 30 feet deep. In the evening they may confine their shoreline visits to ledges that are 6-12 feet deep. So in the daytime deep-running lures are best, and in the evening sub-surface lures are the choice.

More than 80°: Largemouth settle in cool places beneath lily pads, in holes, or near springs. They are not aggressive or hungry, and have a tendency to toy with food or a lure before taking it. Often it is difficult to feel their nibbles.

Where local regulations permit, night fishing is best during these conditions because in the cool of the evening the bass may rise to the surface for exercise and some food. At that time surface lures such as bass bugs and poppers work best.

Anglers using a thermometer to investigate waters suitable for smallmouth bass should subtract about 5-10° from the foregoing temperatures for largemouth. And they should seek smallmouths in waters with rock, gravel, or sand bottom—not mud.

Blue gills seem most active in water temperatures about 5° higher than a largemouth likes best.

Basic types of equipment

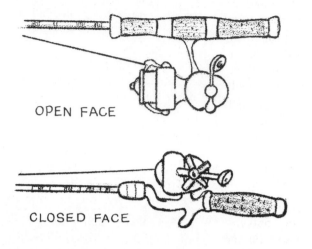

OPEN FACE

CLOSED FACE

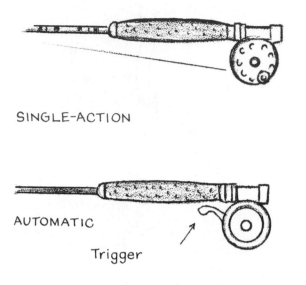

SINGLE-ACTION

AUTOMATIC

Trigger

There are two types of spinning reels—open-face and closed-face. Different size lines can be loaded quickly for different kinds of fishing.

Fly reels are mainly storage spools for line. The automatic fly reel, which retrieves line with a spring mechanism, is a favorite for use in small streams.

Although fish haven't changed much in 40,000,000 years, the equipment to catch them has.

For example, only a few years back the only good rod was a split bamboo rod, and it cost $100 or more. Such a rod still costs that much or more, because it takes skilled craftsmen many tedious hours to select the right kind of imported tonkin cane, cut it into strips, carefully shave, sand, and match the pieces, glue them together, and thus—after several weeks— make a good rod by hand.

Today a man does not have to save a fortune before he can fish with fine equipment. With the benefits of new inventions in materials and manufacturing processes, precision-made glass rods with much the same type of $100 hand-crafted bamboo action are mass-produced to sell at one-fourth the cost.

Reels today are made from new metals invented during our air age. Lightweight miracles of design and engineering, they give a fisherman better line control and more efficiency at new, low costs.

Lines have changed from the former oiled silk and braided linen materials to synthetic fibers such as nylon and dacron. These synthetics are used in two ways. In a transparent form, the line is called monofilament. Also, monofilament cores are coated with a durable plastic to make special lines for certain types of fishing, mainly fly casting.

SPINNING EQUIPMENT

Perfected only a few years ago, and introduced to the United States just after World War II, the spinning rod and reel enable even a beginning fisherman to cast small lures, bait, or artificial flies a good distance with little effort.

The phenomenal public acceptance of spinning equipment can be explained easily by listing the advantages this method gives a fisherman.

1. Easy casting. The technique of spin casting can be mastered in a short time because there is no problem of backlash in the reel, which avoids many line tangles (called "bird's nests" in polite society). Neither are there any complicated tricks or skills to be acquired for getting the lure into the water. All the angler need do is hold the rod and throw the lure from its tip, and watch the slack in his line so it doesn't get tangled in the reel handle or some other projection.

2. Adaptability. Spin casting gear can be used for all types of freshwater fishing since line sizes can be changed quickly by installing a new spool with a different line. Therefore, one outfit can accommodate many lures and sinkers for a wide variety of conditions.

3. Low cost. At the low price of spinning equipment, an average family can easily afford to own more than one outfit.

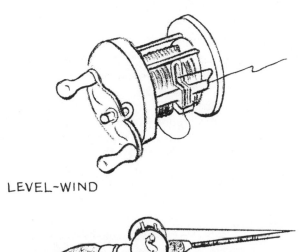

LEVEL-WIND

The level-wind reel is especially good for trolling. It is also good for casting ⅜ to ⅝ ounce lures or sinkers. This plug-caster's favorite has a brake for line tension.

PRINCIPLE OF SPIN CASTING

When casting a spinning lure, momentum created by the weight of a tiny lure is what pulls the line out. As the fisherman readies himself for a cast he flexes or bends his rod to set the lure in motion with a snap of the wrist. Casts can be made overhead, sidearm, or from any other position. The technique is that uncomplicated.

The basic reason spin casting is so different from fly casting or plug casting is that the reel spool does not revolve. Instead the line uncoils off a fixed spool with practically no resistance. And since the spool does not turn it does not wind the line into a tangle of backlash.

There are two types of spinning reels. The open-face reel has the line spool exposed. It fits under the rod handle. As the user holds his rod in his right hand he winds the handle of the open-face reel with his left (or vice versa with some models).

The closed-face spinning reel operates on the same fixed-spool principle, but the spool is housed in metal and is on top of the rod instead of on the bottom. With this reel, when the angler plays a fish, he holds his rod conventionally with his left hand and winds the handle with his right. This is similar to the favorite old American plug casting method for retrieving a line.

Those who like close-in fishing often prefer the closed-face reel. They reason that the spool is better-protected from damage, and they also enjoy the advantages of greater mechanical control, which many enthusiasts say it offers.

Fishermen who enjoy making long, accurate casts with light lures generally choose the open-face reel because there is less friction, and they like the right-hand control of the rod as they reel in with their left.

Potential buyers should visit any tackle store and examine the two types of spinning reels before they decide which will suit them best.

DRAG BRAKE

Spinning reels are equipped with a device called a drag brake. This is a mechanical contrivance which works on the friction principle. It provides braking power on the line as the fish pulls it out, and can be adjusted easily while fighting a fish. Its action makes fighting fish drag the line from the reel as it battles to get free. Whereas fly and plug casting equipment may require expert finger manipulation to land a large fish, the spinning fisherman's drag brake accomplishes the same job mechanically.

Before casting, the fisherman should set his drag by tightening it to the degree he thinks necessary for the kind of fish he seeks, and to maneuver the size line he intends to use without breaking it or tearing the hook out of the fish's mouth.

He tests his adjustment by pulling the line to learn how much effort he must exert to get the line off the reel. This should be considerably less than the effort required to break the line in two.

Then he is ready to cast. The drag, or brake adjustment—should the first guess be wrong—is located where the forefinger or thumb of the hand holding the rod can reach it quickly.

FLY ROD EQUIPMENT

Fly casting is the traditional way of fishing among experts who believe that when a man reaches a point where he understands how to fish, he should adopt the most sporting way of doing it. If he can still fill his creel under that handicap, then he has earned his right to be called expert.

A fly rod is similar to a long spring, and the basic principle of fly-casting is that the springiness of the rod tip does the work of sending the line on its way. As the line shoots out, it carries the fly. The most popular rod among veteran fly casters is one that has most of its springy action in the tip section. The best all-around rod is one designed for easy 30-40-foot casting with a fairly light tapered line.

For this reason, rod and line must be matched. A light line doesn't bend a stiff rod enough to give it good action. Conversely, a heavy line will give a limber-shafted rod an overload and it will not handle properly.

The fly reel is not too important. Its primary function is as a storage place for line. It is made as simply as possible for the purpose.

DRY-FLY RIG

Dry-fly fishermen are interested in catching fish with an artificial fly that floats on the water's surface, and they use a tapered line and leader for casting. This is a line which decreases gradually in diameter at its end. When cast properly, the belly weight of the line carries the tapered line-end and tapered leader through the air. As the rig reaches the end of its casting loop, the line straightens and drops the fly on the water with amazing naturalness.

WET-FLY RIG

A wet-fly fisherman seeks fish beneath the surface. He may do it with a fast-sinking fly line designed to carry a lure below the surface with its own weight. He can use a regular fly line and maneuver it in a way to make it sink. He may choose to add a coating of mud to make it sink. In some cases he may attach a tiny sinker about five feet from the hook.

PLUG-CASTING EQUIPMENT

This equipment was at its peak of popularity when spin casting was introduced. Then it declined, but is now regaining favor.

The greatest advantage of plug-casting (or bait-casting) equipment is that it can also be used for fishing from a moving boat (trolling). With today's growing interest in boats and lakes, there are many occasions when an angler needs an outfit which is the right size, weight, and shape for trolling, and which can also be used for casting a variety of baits. With a little practice a man can become a deadly caster with this rig, and a successful fish-getter, so it is excellent equipment to own, especially for a man who has a boat.

The plug outfit is also well suited for fishing in smaller lakes or ponds where bass live among weeds and other obstructions that cause mild snags. The strength of the equipment enables a fisherman to pull through the stuff without losing expensive gear. Also, it is perfect for casting plugs, spoons, or sinkers which are too heavy for spinning equipment.

The plug rod is four to six feet long, and although lightweight is strong. The reel is called a level-wind reel because it has a contrivance which automatically distributes the line evenly on the spool as the fisherman winds it in.

The size line used on a plug-casting reel is in the 15 to 24-pound test range.

The tackle box

Between the distant ends of a fishing outfit— the rod butt and the bait in the water—there is a conglomeration of big and little gadgets and pieces which help catch fish when they are not causing disorder in the bottom of a creel, tackle box, or pocket. The following is a list of leaders, sinkers, and other items every fisherman should have.

LEADERS

There are two general types of leaders, the almost-invisible (to a fish) short pieces of line to which hooks are fixed. One is made of fine, transparent nylon measuring from 3 to 12 feet. A tapered type is used for fly casting and level monofilament works well for bait fishing with light sinkers. The other type leader is a short connection, about 9 to 12 inches, between line and lure. Made of abrasion-resistant material such as fine wire or heavy nylon, its purpose is to resist cutting from rocks or a fish's teeth.

Here are suggested leader sizes for tackle box storage:

Tapered leaders: 5X or 1 lb. test, for trout to 10 inches: 4X or 1½ lb. test, for trout 10 to 12 inches; 3X or 2½ lb. test for trout more than 14 inches.

Level leaders: 3 spools of monofilament line measuring 2 lb., 4 lb., and 8 lb. test. These are tied to heavier line to serve as leaders. They are called "tippets."

Short leaders: Heavy nylon or fine, flexible wire materials are available at tackle shops. When custom-made, the short leader is equipped with a swivel on one end and a snap on the other.

Top row, left to right, are dipsey, sleeve, pencil sinkers, then two other dipsey shapes. Lower left is a swivel. To its right a snap. BB sinkers, several types of hooks, leaders, small first aid packets are other necessities.

SWIVELS

A swivel is an attachment between line and leader. It has an eyelet at each end; these revolve freely inside a tiny barrel, allowing a lure to rotate without twisting the line. Number 10 or No. 12 swivels are used for average casts with bait or spinners for trout. Number 7 or No. 5 are larger, and best suited for plug casting for bass or for trolling from a boat.

SNAPS

A snap works on the safety pin principle. It can be snapped to the eyelet of a lure quickly. This eliminates untying and re-tying knots. Snaps are used with large-size spinners and with plugs, never with flies or small lures. When trolling, use them in tandem with a swivel. Sizes Nos. 1, 2, and 3 are best for freshwater.

SINKERS

There are a great many different types of sinkers. Each one is designed for a special purpose. The following are widely useful:

BB or buck shot: These are lead pellets with a slit in one side. The slit is fitted to the line or leader. When the slit is squeezed shut the sinker is fixed to the line. A man can use as many as he wants to establish the desired weight.

Dipsey: This round sinker with a built-in swivel is a favorite for fishing across bottom either with casts or when trolling. The sinker is tied to the line with easily-broken string or leader material so that the lure "swims" a few inches above it. Its roundness reduces the risk of snag, but if one occurs, the string breaks and the main line with its expensive lure is saved.

The dipsey is also popular among still fishermen.

They anchor it on the bottom, then pull their lines taut so the baited hooks float above the bottom.

Dipsey sinkers range from No. 1 at 3½ ounces to No. 10 at ⅛ ounce.

Sleeve: Sleeve sinkers are long and thin. They have a slot along one side into which the line is laid. Lead "ears" are then bent to clamp the sinker to the line. It is a good design for trolling, or for fishing deep among obstructions where its slim silhouette offers little chance for snagging.

Pencil: This sinker is long and small in diameter. It is tied to the line with thread or lightweight leader. Its advantage is that its long shape allows it to rest on top of rocks which might snag a short, plump sinker like the dipsey. Also, it moves easily when a nibbling fish tugs the line.

Like the dipsey, it can be sacrificed when a snag does occur, thus saving expensive gear.

OTHER SUGGESTIONS

Aside from lures, which are dealt with in the next section, there are a number of handy aids to have in the tackle box.

Knife with sharp blade for cleaning fish.
Nail clipper to snip off leader and line ends.
Adhesive tape, always handy in emergencies.
Bandages and disinfectant for first aid.
Mosquito repellent.
Sun glasses.
Spool of red thread to tie bait to hook.
Oil or graphite for lubricating.
Fly dope, to make lures float or sink.
Can opener, which is widely useful.
Repair kit to mend rubber boots, waders.

Rod, reel, and line are only means to an end, which is getting bait into the water where fish will have a try at eating it. Fishermen are often confused about the meaning of terms such as bait, lure, live bait, fresh bait, and artificials.

Actually, any bait is a lure, and vice versa. However, since bait fishing and lure fishing are distinct types the terminology will be defined for purposes of clarity in this book.

Henceforth, the term bait will be used to describe any natural food used to bait a hook. This includes live bait such as worms, hellgrammites, or shrimp, and dead bait such as salmon eggs, sliced chunks of fish, pork rind, or other inanimate food.

Bait is usually the easiest way to attract fish, because it smells good and it tastes good, and a fish will greedily swallow it and the hook if the fisherman presents it well.

The term lures will be used to describe an artificial bait. A lure can be an imitation of a water insect, animal life, small fly, or small fish. Flies, spoons, spinners, and plugs are the lures most commonly used. In this case, it is the task of the fisherman to create an illusion in the fish's brain that will cause him to strike at the lure, which has neither smell nor taste, but only appears appetizing or interesting.

WORMS AND BUGS AND SUCH

Although worms and other small animal forms that creep, hop, or crawl are regarded as baits that seem to work anywhere, they have their limitations.

It would seem logical for worms to work best in early season. At this time of year their bodies are firm, shiny, and full of wriggling life. Fish should not be surprised to find them washed from a bank into the water.

However, in summertime the fish can become suspicious at seeing a worm because the latter just do not travel or go swimming in July. Also, the worm's body in the warm season can be dull, mushy, and unappetizing unless they are specially prepared by keeping them in cool moss or sand to scour their bodies while they feed on corn meal, powdered milk, and coffee grounds to restore themselves for fishing. Good bait and tackle shops sell well-conditioned worms throughout the fishing season.

To be attractive, a worm should be attached to the hook so it stays alive and can act naturally. The best system is to fish it so it looks as though it has accidentally found its way into a stream or lake, and is struggling to find a way out of that environment. In

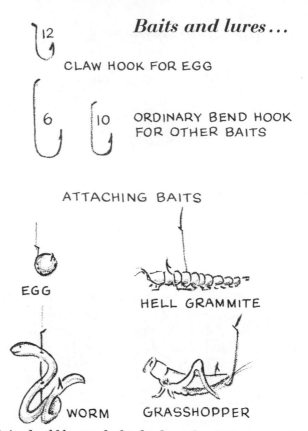

Baits and lures...

CLAW HOOK FOR EGG

ORDINARY BEND HOOK FOR OTHER BAITS

ATTACHING BAITS

EGG

HELL GRAMMITE

WORM

GRASSHOPPER

Baits should be attached to hooks so they behave naturally as they drift on water or beneath the surface.

other words, a smart fisherman works on the worm's instinct to survive in order to fool the fish he is seeking.

The cleverest users of hellgrammites, grasshoppers, fresh water shrimp, minnows, and other varieties of live baits also try to attach them to hooks in ways that allow them to behave as naturally as possible.

Meat or fish chunks do not get the good results with freshwater fish that they do with saltwater varieties. Catfish are an exception. They will eat anything that can't eat them.

SALMON EGGS

Although salmon eggs are inactive and have no life, they should be attached to the hook so they can bounce and drift realistically with the currents. This is true in lakes as well as streams because lakes do have minor up-and-down currents caused by water temperature changes. These drifts affect the behavior of a small egg. Fish prefer to strike at things which do not seem to have strings attached.

A major decision the salmon egg fisherman has to make is choice of color and type. Salmon eggs come in singles or clusters, and are colored white, pink, red, and fluorescent red. They are packed in a variety

...the essential tools

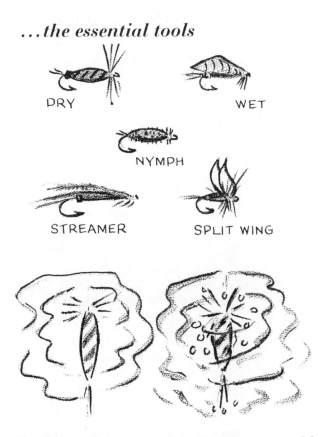

DRY   WET

NYMPH

STREAMER   SPLIT WING

Dry flies, of all types, must be well-made to attract fish. Good job floats as at lower left; poor one as at right.

of preservatives which can make the egg texture vary from soft to hard.

Some fishermen say that if a trout is stung by the hook in a pink egg it will refuse another egg of the same color, but may strike at a white or red egg. So it is a good idea to have two or more colors on hand.

Regardless of color, the egg should be firm enough to hold its place on the hook, or at least firm enough that a loose turn of red thread will keep it in place. Many fish refuse salmon eggs because the hook has revealed itself.

ARTIFICIAL FLIES

Artificial flies are one of the world's oldest and most successful lures. They come in four general classifications: Dry, wet, nymph, and streamer.

The dry fly rests on the surface, to resemble a floating insect.

The wet fly is used beneath the surface, to look like a submerged insect or a tiny fish.

The nymph is made to resemble an immature insect living on the bottom of a lake or stream.

The streamer, when wet, has long feathers and hackles arranged to make it look like a small fish.

Regardless of what fly a fisherman uses, his first job is to deliver it in a way that makes the fish think it is the real thing. Therefore, the imitation must be made from good materials. After that come size and color. (The sketch left gives a rough idea of what a fish sees when he looks at good flies and poor ones.)

A dry fly of good quality has stiff hackles which do not break the surface tension of the water. The fly floats high-up on its hackle points, creating an interesting silhouette and minimizing the number of air bubbles and other distractions which may frighten away a fish. It is as nearly natural-looking as an artificial fly can be.

A dry fly of poor quality has soft hackles which become soggy after use. This fly must depend largely upon its body wrap to keep it afloat. When a fish looks up, he sees a mass of air bubbles surrounding an unfamiliar object instead of a familiar insect. There also may be evidences of water drag caused by poor construction. The fish will not bite. In many cases he will not even bother to swim toward the lure.

The Westerner's fly box should always include Gray Hackle with Yellow body to imitate the prolific May fly; Brown Hackle with Peacock body to imitate mosquitoes and other brown fly families; Royal Coachman, which is a wildly colored fly featuring white wings and which gets results the world over; Black Gnat to resemble dark insects; and a few others to carry for luck. Hook sizes should be Nos. 10, 12, and 14.

SPINNERS

The spinner is a device that attracts attention with a blade that rotates in the water. It is a fisherman's advertising gimmick to get customers, namely fish.

The average stream fisherman carries an assortment of spinners which he occasionally uses to substitute for bait, spoon, or fly. He likes having a variety of lures on his person because they give him a change of pace. They may add fish to his creel.

The choice of color—silver, brass, bronze, copper, or black, or some combination of these—depends upon the water clarity, time of day, and habits of the fish. There is no set formula for color selection, and fishermen are best advised to experiment until they find the color and spinner size that does the job.

The oscillation and flash of the spinner blade may cause a fish to think it is a minnow, something to play with, or an object to strike in anger.

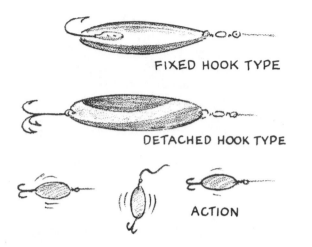

FIXED HOOK TYPE

DETACHED HOOK TYPE

ACTION

Spoons are lures of polished or painted metal which produce the action of darting or injured small fish.

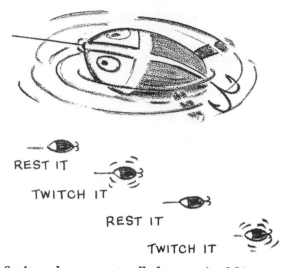

REST IT

TWITCH IT

REST IT

TWITCH IT

Surface plugs are naturally buoyant for fishing near the surface. Slight tugs on the line make them twitch.

Spinners are used in naked style, with only hooks attached, or are used ahead of other lures such as streamer flies or bait (worms) to call attention to the latter.

SPOONS

The spoon gets its name for resembling the oval shape of an ordinary tablespoon or teaspoon. It is a favorite in lakes and has a wobbling action in the water which also gives it the nickname, "wobbler."

There are two general types of spoons: 1) the fixed-hook spoon which races and darts, and 2) the wobbler spoon with free-swinging hook, which imitates the action of an injured fish. The first type is fished rapidly to give it speedy, get-away action. The second type is worked slowly.

Also in the spoon family are lures not shaped like a spoon, but which have a wobbling type action.

There should be a selection of spoons or wobblers in every boat fisherman's tackle box. The accepted colors are orange, silver, chrome, and white for murky waters or overcast days. Gold, or combinations of bronze-and-red or red-and-white are used on 'sunny, clear days.

The average fisherman will find sizes up to ½ ounce are sufficient for any type fishing from spin casting to trolling.

PLUGS

The plug was developed for catching black bass in

lakes. Newer, smaller ones are used extensively for trout fishing in streams and lakes. Plugs are usually carved or molded lures with a body that resembles a small fish. Plugs are shaped to give darting or wobbling action. Metal plates and plastic scoops are sometimes added for diving and depth capability. There are three main types—surface, sub-surface, and deep-running. Each has its place, depending on conditions.

Surface plugs: These plugs are buoyant and ride high on the surface. An important factor in their design is silhouette, because shape is important to fish as they look up.

Another important feature to look for in surface plugs is their noise production. Surface fishing gets best results at dusk and often a little extra noise is an attention getter, especially with bass. To create noise, surface plugs are sometimes equipped with a propellor blade or a concave head which helps them pop or jump in a noisy manner. Hungry fish that have been lying in the weeds all day frequently jump at these noisy plugs—whether in anger or out of hunger no fisherman can ever be sure.

Sub-surface plugs: These plugs float when at rest. When retrieved, their body design, or metal or plastic scoops force them beneath the surface. The faster they are retrieved, the deeper they are driven.

Sub-surface plugs offer a wide variety of actions, not only from the built-in design of the lure, but also from the way the fisherman works his rod and line. They can be made to dart, dive, rise, fall, or wobble weakly. They are especially effective on bright, breezy days when fish leave the shallows for deeper water,

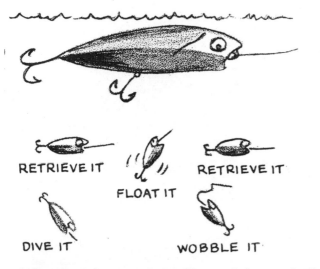

Sub-surface plugs are designed to work best at depths from 1 to 10 feet. Speed of retrieve determines depth.

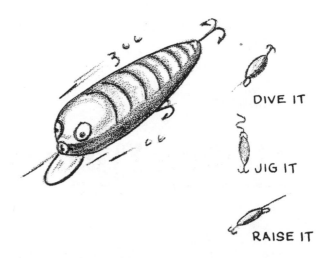

Deep-running plugs sink of their own weight. They are designed for deep-water, midday fishing.

and the chop of the surface disguises the line.

Deep-running plugs: These plugs have little buoyancy. They are built with lead weights to sink quickly. They are used mostly in deep water during midday.

FRUIT SALAD

Sporting goods dealers carry many strange devices which fishermen buy to catch fish under special circumstances. Sometimes the angler is successful. Sometimes he is not.

Perhaps the oddest of all these gadgets is the western lake trolling rig called a "fruit salad." It is a highly ornamental, two-bladed attractor outfit. Known also as a "Christmas tree" the contraption is a killer, and is used only by fishermen who are not going to catch anything otherwise, and need to do something desperate to avoid an empty creel.

The rig is made up of wire measuring 30 inches, with several inches of bright red beads at either end. Attached to one end is a shiny 5-inch spinning blade, and to the other a 3-inch blade. The line is attached to the big spinner's assembly, and a 12-inch leader is attached at the small spinner assembly.

A healthy common angleworm is fixed to a No. 4 worm hook, and the entire contraption is thrown overboard, and trolled at a depth of 20 to 50 feet. The theory is that few fish can resist a swim toward such a thing. As the fish approaches (almost always from the front or side), he watches the parade go by, until he sees a nice, juicy worm trailing along. Then temptation overrides judgment, and the fish takes the worm.

LEARN TO USE EQUIPMENT

Regardless of the kind of equipment a fisherman owns, or what a friend recommends, the most important thing is to use the gear correctly.

Before going fishing, a man should study and practice with a dummy plug or hookless fly at home. A lawn or driveway offers a good casting area where tackle familiarity can be developed.

There, if he creates a line tangle, snaps off a lure, or doesn't cast accurately, he has time to work it out. He doesn't have to fight the impatience that possesses a fisherman at water's edge and causes him to compound his frustrating errors.

If possible, he should visit an angling club where members can help him learn the correct art of casting and handling a lure. Members of these groups are often anxious to help apprentice fishermen because this builds supporters for the art of fishing, and perhaps future members.

At streamside he might ask the advice of known experts and listen attentively to what they have to say. Too often a man is inclined to make a long explanatory speech about what he thinks is his trouble instead of asking a simple question that might bring a helpful answer.

A fisherman should not look like an overstocked sporting goods store. He should be well prepared, but to impress fish, not fishermen.

When hiking to a lake, or along a stream, the angler should carry as little equipment as possible. Heavy loads are not only awkward and hard to keep track of, they also put a strain on the patience and heart.

Fishing Western Streams

When a Westerner thinks about fishing in a stream, the picture that comes to his mind is often of a swift, narrow ribbon of water coursing along a clean, boulder-strewn bed.

This kind of large creek or small river occurs in the great, granite mountains of the West far more frequently than does the slow, wandering river that typifies the flatter East and Midwest.

It is the kind of water that produces scrappy trout. It is also the kind of water that makes a fisherman work hard at his art. The pace is fast, and usually the water is clear enough for fish to notice an angler's mistakes.

Bait fishing in a stream

If a person taking up fishing hopes to graduate from beginner to the expert class he should start by catching fish. To catch them he should use the lure fish will bite most readily.

In most cases this is bait, in egg, worm, or other juicy form. Because fish have a sense of taste, they are more inclined to take and eat real food than they are the make-believe variety. There are exceptions, of course, such as when fish rise to certain kinds of flies. In such cases an angler should be equipped to meet the situation.

So a good way to start learning how to fish a stream is to use bait because, as a hungry fish gulps it, he almost always swallows the hook. And when a trout is hooked firmly in the mouth or throat there isn't much chance for him to get away unless the line or leader breaks. The fisherman should not rule out using artificials also, such as flies and spinners. Sometimes they work better than any genuine food.

Later, the novice can adopt (we hope) the more difficult and skillful ways of fishing, such as using flies and very light tackle. At this time, if he achieves success, he is entitled to take a few bows because by hard work and perseverance he has graduated into the ranks of expert. He has learned to outwit the fish under a variety of conditions with equipment that gives a fighting fish a good chance to break away.

But at the beginning, the sport of stream fishing must be learned. And if the first attempts are disappointing, the prospective angler may turn to other sports and miss out on the real thrill a good catch can bring.

The purpose of this chapter, then, is to explain the basic steps a novice should take in preparing himself for fishing a stream. After he digests this, he will find he is more likely to get some understanding help from experienced friends fishing nearby.

THE BASIC EQUIPMENT

Either the spinning, fly, or plug-casting equipment can be used for bait fishing in a stream. Each has certain advantages.

Spinning equipment with a 4-pound test line is best to start with but since spinning equipment is fully described in the sections on shore fishing in lakes, fly rod equipment will serve here as the main example for bait fishing in a stream.

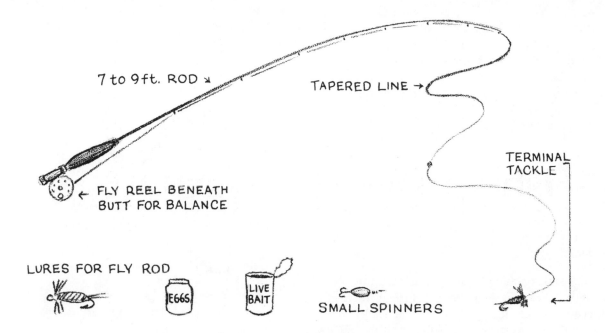

7 to 9ft. ROD

TAPERED LINE →

TERMINAL
TACKLE

← FLY REEL BENEATH
BUTT FOR BALANCE

LURES FOR FLY ROD

E66S

LIVE
BAIT

SMALL SPINNERS

The fly rod is long and slender, with great springiness in its tip section. This springiness helps to tire out a gamefish quickly on very light tackle.

The fly rod is long and limber. The springiness of the shaft puts a great deal of action at the rod tip to help cast the line, set the hook, and play the fish in a way that tires him.

The reel is simplicity in itself. Its primary function is the storage of line.

The line may be a tapered or level casting line finished in slick, enamel-like plastic of the sinking or non-floating type. Or it may be transparent nylon monofilament.

For close-in bait fishing with a fly rod within a radius of about 20 to 50 feet, the new sinking fly line is a good choice. Slick, with a small diameter, it offers little resistance to the water and is easy to use. As with the monofilament, it behaves more naturally in the water than other types of casting lines, and it sinks faster so the bait can get to deep water quicker.

Attached to it is a 4-foot leader of tiny monofilament measuring about 3-pound test. In low, clear water, the leader might be as long as nine feet.

A sinking type fly line or a 20-pound test monofilament line also has just enough firmness in it to show a line hesitation, or twitch, which a good fisherman always watches for as he has his line in the water. When it happens, it is a good sign that a fish may be nosing the bait. It prepares the angler to set the hook.

Lighter lines are either too fine or too limber to telegraph the nosing activity of a curious fish. Heavier lines resist the water and sometimes scare the fish. So a small diameter fly line or a monofilament line

ranging from 15 to 25-pound test is best for bait fishing with a fly rod.

An added advantage in using a fly line is in the fact that if bait doesn't work the outfit is already rigged to tie on a fly and work it.

TERMINAL TACKLE

The leader, sinker, and hook form the terminal tackle. It should be as lightweight as possible.

Four feet of 3-pound test leader material or about a 5-foot tapered leader measuring 4X is tied to the line. The line-leader combination generally does a good job because the lightweight leader is long enough to float naturally, but still short enough to allow the angler to have proper line control.

In clear water, when fish are seen to approach the bait and then refuse it, a smaller and longer leader may be a better choice because the heavier job may be making the fish wary.

A hook should always be the smallest size a fisherman thinks will hook and hold his catch. The bait should cover the entire hook except for the barb tip because if a fish can see too much hook he is inclined to refuse it and swim away.

For salmon egg bait fishing the best choice is the size No. 12 Claw type. An egg can properly cover this hook and hold its position well. It is more important to cover the hook's eye than its pointed barb.

While fishing, the angler should frequently examine his hook to make sure it is well covered. Eggs that are too soft and mushy are not advisable because they do not hold their place on the hook. The best egg is one with a tender but firm texture that does a good job of concealing and holding its position. A soft egg is preferable to a dried or hard egg.

Hooks for use with worms and crustaceans should range from sizes No. 6 to No. 12. The best hooks for a worm are sizes No. 8 or No. 10 worm hooks. Here the worm should be hooked loosely so it will have a good drifting appearance. Hiding the hook completely with a worm is not nearly so important as it is with a salmon egg.

The sinker should be as light in weight as possible. In most cases, one split shot is sufficient. It should be squeezed so it is firmly placed on the leader, but free enough so the fisherman can still slide it up and down. This is important because it allows the angler to slide the sinker to within 8 inches of the hook for casting into fast water where he wants the bait to get down quickly— or to slide it up as much as 3 feet from the hook for working a deep pool where he wants the bait to flow naturally.

Getting down to business

With fly rod equipment a bait cannot be cast long distances. However, in the kind of stream a beginner enjoys most, which is 15 to 30 feet wide, many excellent spots can be found where it is not necessary to reach far out. Good fishing spots are often within 10 to 20 feet of a caster. Also, by working his rod and line to allow current to take his line downstream, an angler can let out line to fish as far as 100 feet.

The most important thing for him to do after rigging his outfit is to select his fishing spots according to the outline described in the chapter, "Reading a stream."

APPROACHING A FISHING SPOT

When approaching a fishing spot, a man's progress should be slow and he should try to blend himself into the landscape.

Fish are suspicious of unusual movement, noise, color or shadows, and a cautious approach to a stream reduces the chance of scaring the fish. See the section on a fish's vision, on page 8.

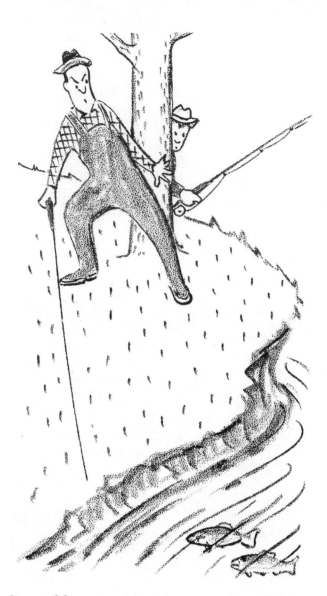

Stream fish are suspicious characters. An angler's approach to them must be cautious and quiet.

THE CAST

After the fisherman has selected his spot, baited his hook, and is ready to fish, he strips 30 feet of line from his fly reel to ready himself for a smooth cast with a round-house, sweeping motion. He uses this method for two reasons. It doesn't jerk the bait off his hook in mid-air, and it allows the bait to land on the water softly without changing its position on the hook.

WATCH THE LINE

As soon as the bait settles in the water, the primary interest of the fisherman becomes one of watching the

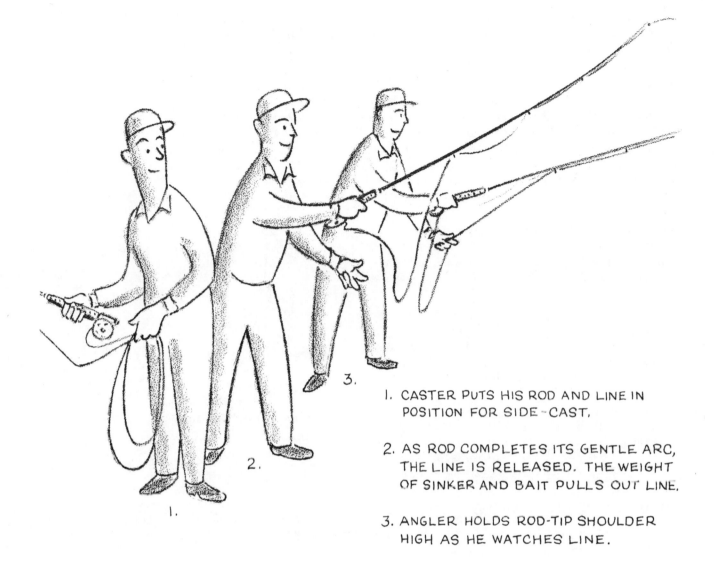

1. CASTER PUTS HIS ROD AND LINE IN POSITION FOR SIDE-CAST.

2. AS ROD COMPLETES ITS GENTLE ARC, THE LINE IS RELEASED. THE WEIGHT OF SINKER AND BAIT PULLS OUT LINE.

3. ANGLER HOLDS ROD-TIP SHOULDER HIGH AS HE WATCHES LINE.

The bait cast with a fly-rod (or any other type of rod) is a smooth, sweeping action. This roundhouse motion reduces the chance of dislodging bait from the hook.

behavior of his line. A good angler never takes his eyes off it because watching the line's behavior gives his eyes information which his fingers may not feel. For example, if he notices that his line hesitates or twitches he can be reasonably sure a fish is mouthing or nosing his bait. He may not feel the action, but he can see it.

HAND POSITIONS

The fisherman's hand positions as he watches his line are important. The right hand holds the rod so the tip is fairly low, about shoulder high. The left hand holds a loop of line between thumb and forefinger.

If he sees a line hesitation that may indicate a fish,

he may not strike immediately, but instead lower his rod tip to let line slip out from the loop in his left hand. This line slack allows the fish to continue playing with the bait without feeling its attachment to a line. There is no suspicious give-away to make him think what he is going to eat has a hook in it. As a consequence, he may take a firmer hold on the bait. When he does, that is the time for the angler to try to set his hook.

RETRIEVING LINE

With a fly rod — or any other casting equipment — the process of retrieving line begins almost as soon as the bait or lure settles on the water.

A man using fly rod equipment and bait will retrieve line by the process known as "mending." That means bringing line in with one hand, and storing excess loops in the crook of the forefinger of the other (rod-holding) hand.

The technique differs slightly with different baits and lures. A man using bait has to remember to make his bait "work" for him under water. As he brings line in, he should make the line twitch and hesitate if he is using hellgrammites, worms, or some other animated creature. This will make it seem as though the bait is trying to get out of the water. A man using salmon eggs is more concerned to make it look as though nothing at all is interfering with the regular action of the current, so he tries to make his line match the speed and direction of the water as it flows smoothly over gravel bottom, or churns around obstructions.

The important thing is to remember to reduce the amount of line in the water while the bait floats or drifts downstream past the angler. The critical point is reached as the line straightens downstream, because at this time the man has to be able to lift the bait from the water to prepare for a new cast without alarming the fish. The total amount of line out should not be much more than the combined length of rod and fisherman. That way, the lure can be lifted clear of the surface and brought inshore without splashing along the surface, or having to be towed back upstream.

FISHING UPSTREAM AND DOWNSTREAM

The two most popular methods of bait fishing in a stream are:

(1) to choose a pool or pocket and drop the bait into that area. There it is allowed to lie quietly or float leisurely with the current. The fisherman hopes a trout looking for food along the bottom will swallow the hook, or

(2) the other method is to fish the current. Here the fisherman uses a light sinker. He gets best results by casting a short distance upstream and allowing his bait to float toward him, over underwater rocks, logs, or shelves which may hide fish.

As the bait travels downstream he tries to handle his line in a way that will eliminate drag or unnatural floating of the bait. As the line begins to straighten out he works his bait carefully and is especially alert because this is a period when a fish may strike. He retrieves his bait slowly and then makes another cast upstream to repeat the maneuver.

Few fish are caught by casting bait downstream and holding the line taut against the current.

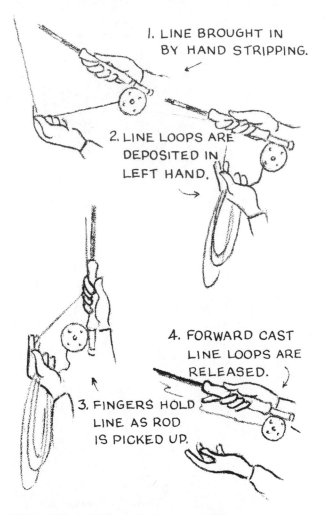

1. LINE BROUGHT IN BY HAND STRIPPING.

2. LINE LOOPS ARE DEPOSITED IN LEFT HAND.

3. FINGERS HOLD LINE AS ROD IS PICKED UP.

4. FORWARD CAST LINE LOOPS ARE RELEASED.

When fly-rod fishing, the line is stored in the fingers rather than the reel, the reverse of spinning technique.

A popular approach to bait fishing is to cast up or across stream, then to guide bait naturally along stream bottom.

WRONG

RIGHT

A valuable secret for hooking fish: The WRONG way is lifting the rod butt. This puts an arc in rod's tip, creating a slack line. RIGHT way is to push the rod butt down, as shown at right. This motion raises the tip of the rod, creating taut line.

STRIKING

The art of hooking a fish properly requires the same kind of precision and timing a golfer needs for delicate approach shots, a shotgunner uses for snap shots at birds, or a baseball pitcher needs to get the ball where he wants it.

The better a fisherman is the more he seems to realize that he can lose his timing when he doesn't practice and fish. Some men claim that after several months away from fishing it may take several hours or maybe several days to recapture the reflexes and timing that hook fish.

Another problem is that the timing and method of striking can vary in different streams because native fish have different eating habits. For example, a rainbow trout living in a stream bordering a rich pasture may be used to seeing worms that come from the soil, so he will hit them quickly. On the other hand, a rainbow living in a granite bottom stream where worms are scarce may be suspicious when he sees a wriggling thing in front of his nose. He may watch it carefully before taking it—if he ever does.

Therefore, a worm fisherman must strike in two different ways. In the pasture stream he acts quickly to hook the fish whereas in the granite bottom stream he lets the cagy fish play with the bait so as to encourage his getting careless about the hook inside it.

TOP SECRET

Perhaps the most surprising thing to fishermen who have trouble hooking fish is to learn that a fish is hooked best by pushing the rod butt down instead of raising it. The sketch above shows the behavior of the rod tip under these two different actions. Many fish are lost because the angler doesn't understand this technique of getting the most out of his equipment.

When netting a stream fish, the angler's first job is to find secure footing. Then he leads the fish headfirst to the net, holding the rod high to give himself extra line.

LANDING A STREAM FISH

A fly rod with its long, slim shaft has a springy strength and deadly action for landing a trout that tires a fish quicker than other rods.

A skilled user of a fly rod exerts steady pressure that never lets up. He never allows the fish to find slack line so he can throw the hook, or to get a solid purchase so he can break line or leader, and thus become a successful escapee.

There are two ways of handling the fly rod while landing a fish. For fish approximately 14 inches and under, an experienced angler will favor the method of hand-stripping the line. After the hook is set he uses his left hand to strip in line while holding the rod in his right. Stripped line is held in the crook of the right forefinger, as with the retrieve noted earlier. This method is continued until the fish is landed. It is quick, direct, and features positive control.

The other method, generally for large fish, is to bring the rod back enough to put a gentle bend in it. If right-handed, the angler then transfers his rod to his left hand, holding the line taut by pressing it between left forefinger and rod. Quickly he winds any slack line onto his reel. With that chore done, he fishes by manipulating his reel, bringing in or letting out line as he feels the challenge demands.

In playing the fish, the fly rod angle should range between 45 and 65° from horizontal. When the fish jumps the rod is manipulated to keep a slight, steady bend in the shaft.

One exception is when the line is deep in the water where water resistance added to line pull may put a breaking strain on the line. This often happens with salmon and steelhead. The other case is when a fish jumps away from the fisherman. Here a taut line may cause the fish to fall on the line and break it as he re-enters the water. In either situation the rod tip should be lowered to give the fish some room to move.

When landing a fish from a stream, the angler has two choices. The safest is to work the fish toward shore and beach him. The other is to use a landing net, the only choice in mid-stream.

In both cases the fish must be steered clear of obstructions, and should never be forced, or "horsed in."

When netting, the rod is held in the left hand, with the left arm well back, up and over the shoulder (as in the sketch above). With an extended right arm, the right hand holds the entire net submerged. When the fish is led to a point over the net — head first — the net is raised around him.

To kill trout quickly, bend the head back. Take a big fish to shore before removing the hook. Many fine prizes escape because they squirt from an angler's hands into the water.

The Purist's Approach...fishing with artificial flies

A fly purist is an experienced fisherman who loves the game of outwitting a wily fish with an artificial fly. He refuses to carry spinners, flashing devices, or bait (or at least refuses to carry them where they can be seen) because he thinks the artificial fly challenges his skills to the highest degree and is therefore the most sporting lure to use.

When he goes fishing the fly expert prefers to rely upon his own observations of a stream to decide which fly to use. To him, relying upon the recommendations of a dealer or some other vacationer is a hit-and-miss procedure. He may be correct, and then again he may not. But in any case, he is intensely proud of his art, and an addition to any conversation about fishing. A man who wants to fish with artificial flies first has to decide which one to use.

HOW EXPERTS CHOOSE A FLY

LIFT SOME STONES. Study insect life found beneath rocks in stream bed. Choose a fly to match color and size (hook size). This is best for nymph fishing.

STUDY THE CURRENTS. Walk around a pool to see what kinds of food are floating in the stream. Fish have a tendency to feed on the food that is most plentiful at the moment, and also at the stream depth where most food is. Wet-fly men do this, not only to guide fly selection, but to decide how deep to work their flies.

LOOK UNDERNEATH COVER. Look carefully among underwater cover to find out wing sacs or other evidence that nymphs are getting ready to break their shells and hatch. This will tell the size nymph, and later the fly on which trout will feed.

WATCH FLYING INSECTS. Study the behavior and color of flying insects. If one kind dips and rises close to the water a fair number will drown, and trout will begin to take them. Dry-fly men learn from this.

THERE'S MORE to fly fishing. It follows on the next page...

Choosing the Correct Depth to Fish...
Different Kinds of Artificial Flies

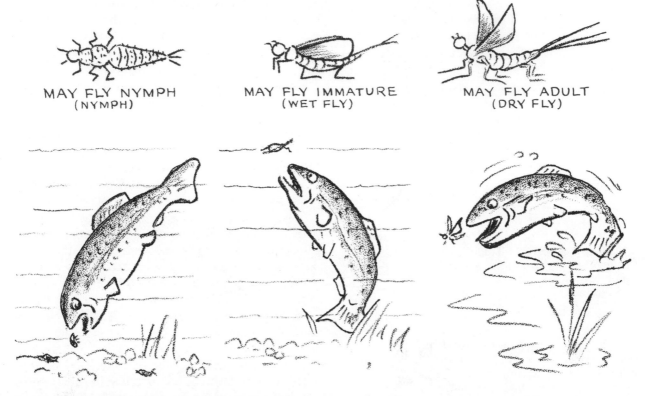

MAY FLY NYMPH
(NYMPH)

MAY FLY IMMATURE
(WET FLY)

MAY FLY ADULT
(DRY FLY)

Different fly techniques work at different times. Using the May fly as an example, fishing the bottom works at nymph stage. Fishing a wet fly near the surface should get fish early in the hatch. Finally, dry flies are a good bet after the hatch.

NYMPH FISHING

A nymph is a form of insect life in the unhatched stage. In protective shells, nymphs are generally found in sand, gravel, or rocks, depending upon the species. Trout regard them as an important part of their diet and continually nose the bottom to reach and eat them. Sometimes trout nosing for nymphs slap the surface with their tails, making fishermen mistakenly think they are surface-feeding.

A nymph imitation is a sparse looking piece of merchandise which looks far from appetizing to a fisherman. But to a trout it can be irresistible. Well-stocked tackle stores carry good selections. One can also be made by snipping or burning off most of the hairy feathers and hackle from an ordinary wet or dry fly.

Nymph fishing is done by casting into a stream with plenty of line paid out so the leader and lure can sink. Some fishermen attach a BB shot 6 to 12 inches above the nymph to help get it down in the water. After a waiting period which may amount to minutes, the fisherman then pulls his nymph across the bottom with very slow retrieves.

The secret is to cause the bait to act erratically and so tantalizingly that a fish will take it, either because of hunger, curiosity, or frustration.

WET-FLY FISHING

The wet fly is an imitation of a water insect leaving its nymph stage. Its action imitates a fly's swim to reach the surface where it can take to the air. Also, it can be an imitation of a small fish.

The best way to fish a wet fly is to cast it across current and let it float freely with the water as insects do.

The critical period frequently comes as the loose

line several times he starts a slow retrieve and prepares for another cast.

Many unlucky fishermen who have decided to give up fishing for a while have walked away from a stream while their line dragged in the water behind them. And they have unexpectedly hooked a fish. The fish hit because the fishermen's walking caused the fly to jig up and down in a tantalizing way. The fish struck the lure so it couldn't get away.

Dead-fly method: To be a good wet-fly fisherman in the slicks and edges of riffles and pools, which are favorite dining rooms for trout, the best overall method is to cast upstream or across stream and allow the line and fly to have a natural drift downstream with the current. This is called the "dead fly" method. The object is to let the fly sink and drift naturally through the promising water.

Live-fly method: The action of "live fly" method is useful in shallower waters where the surface is choppy enough to help disguise the leader. Here, the object is to work the fly among submerged rocks or other obstructions so the trout will mistake it for a small fish. Casts are also made up and across the stream.

Fishing two flies: Many wet-fly fishermen use two flies, one at the tip of the leader and one attached to a leader loop about 2 feet from the tip. The idea is to present two varieties of flies with one cast and thus offer a fish a chance of one or the other. This system may get results in fast or murky water but seldom in medium flowing or clear water.

About the only exception is when the second fly is attached half-way up the leader to act as a floater. In such a case it provides buoyancy to the rig and helps carry the fly at the end of the leader down the current in an enticing way.

When wet-fly fishing, the non-expert will often have his best luck as the line begins to straighten downstream.

line begins to straighten in the stream. This is because trout have an inborn habit of following hatching nymphs and water bugs downstream as the insects seek the surface.

At about a foot below the surface a water insect generally struggles or hesitates a fraction of a second as it makes final preparations to free itself from its watery home and escape to the surface or to the air. Trout know this and have a habit of striking at this time because they don't want the food to get away.

Expert wet-fly fishermen also know about this habit of fish following an insect and striking it just below the surface. Therefore, after casting across a stream the wise angler watches his line straighten. As it does so he works his line to cause his lure to move up and down in the current just below the surface.

If he feels a faint nick or sees his line hesitate he can gamble that a fish is near his lure and he can strike. If he doesn't get any action after working his

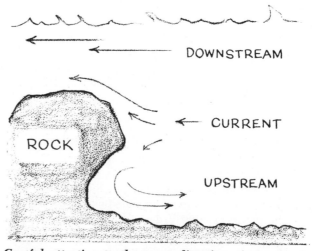

Careful attention to the exact direction of currents is an important part of successful wet-fly technique.

DRY-FLY FISHING

In dry-fly fishing an angler uses an artificial fly made with buoyant types of hackle and hair. It is designed primarily to imitate a natural adult insect floating downstream on the surface.

In the West, where the steep slopes of hills and mountains cause waters to flow fast and the streams are comparatively narrow, the number of good dry fly waters are not so plentiful as they are in the flatter terrain and gentler waters of the Midwest and East.

Perhaps the best Western dry-fly waters are in the high-altitude flatlands and mountain meadows where streams seem to rest as they flow leisurely through a valley. Another good place is in the shallow, choppy waters of thousands of mountain lakes. Dry flies also do well in large streams where the current widens and slows before tumbling into the next pool.

If one were to make a broad statement about where to find good dry-fly fishing in the West it could ·be said that it is generally accomplished best in streams to three feet deep that course over boulders and on lakes near the shore when the surface is choppy.

The aim of dry-fly fishing is to put the fly down gently on the surface of the water so as not to sink it. A tapered line, which has a decreasing diameter at its end, is used to make the cast. The non-expert will get better results by fishing a dry fly on a choppy or rippling surface than he will by trying to lay his fly naturally on a quiet stretch of water. The latter demands a technique that can come only from practice, balanced equipment, and know-how.

When a tapered line and tapered leader are used together, a good caster can drop a fly on the water with amazing naturalness.

The favorite line for dry-fly fishing is a floater, one especially made to float on the surface of the water. A fisherman may prefer to add buoyancy to his fly by treating it with a few dabs of dry-fly oil or silicone dressing although the value of such preparations is subject to debate. Many anglers prefer to tie or to learn how to handle their fly so it will float without benefit of oil or dressing.

The combination of floating line and floating fly gives the fisherman the kind of buoyancy he wants to hook surface feeders.

However, and this is important, the leader should not be treated with any substance that makes it float. On the contrary, the leader should lie beneath the surface to help eliminate any look of attachment to the fly. Some experts rub mud on their leaders to make them sink.

The perfect cast finds the line floating and moving with the surface water so the fisherman can watch it. The fly floats seven to nine feet away from the line at the end of its submerged leader. There is no sign of attachment between the line and hook because the leader is below the surface.

BASIC PRINCIPLES OF DRY-FLY

The basic principles of dry-fly fishing are simple, but perfection in technique and a balanced outfit are required to master them. The fly is cast up and slightly across stream. As it drifts toward the fisherman he picks up slack line with his left hand—and then raises his rod tip to lift the floating fly off the surface. Then he casts again—and again—and again.

A good dry-fly man should learn to use a tiny fly with as small a leader as possible, such as a size 5X.

Frequently trout can be seen jumping in a stream but despite their activity they refuse to take an angler's fly no matter how well he presents it. In many cases the reason is because the fly is too large and the leader too heavy. Many old-timers claim that the heavier a stream is fished the smaller should be the artificial fly to get results.

As a consequence, they frequently use hook sizes ranging down to No. 18. This is a tiny size that puts artificials into the diminutive midge or tiny gnat category. It is difficult to cast and float but when done properly it gets results.

Dry-fly fishermen must also know a variety of casts so they can handle their fly under a variety of conditions. These techniques are best learned at a casting club or along the banks of a river where expert volunteers do some teaching.

But when all is said and done, the dry-fly fisherman should have the attitude that he is stalking the trout. And if he keeps working, moves slowly and quietly, and doesn't offer his body as a frightening silhouette against the sky he will probably catch some fish.

Reading a stream...to find out where the fish are

Before an angler starts fishing, he should study the water and its surroundings. The things he learns may help solve his problem—which is to catch a good mess of fish.

Fishing, along with other sports, has many reading enthusiasts. Anglers "read a stream" to study its conditions; golfers "read a green" to find out how to putt a ball; skeet shooters "read a layout" to get information about prevailing winds and shooting background; boatmen "read the skies" to get weather clues; horse players "read the track" to figure their bets.

Reading is a popular word in sports. It suggests how an outdoorsman uses his eyes and thinking apparatus to reach a decision about how and where to do something specific.

In fishing, the conditions a man "reads" to help him make the right decisions are the flow of currents which carry food; eddies which create food depositories; stream bottoms over which the water can flow erratically; obstructions which provide protective cover for fish; and insects, vegetation, sunshine, temperatures, water clarity, and other factors directly related to the life and welfare of a wary gamefish.

In the rugged terrain of the West there is a complete library of freshwater conditions to give stream readers all the intellectual workout even the most experienced angler can ask for.

Streams come in all sizes. From practical experience, a good western fisherman learns to delay fishing until he has finished his reading exercises. Or, to put it another way, he does his lessons first and catches his fish last.

The following 12 points describe the kind of reading a stream fisherman should do before he wets a line. It is a good even-dozen to remember.

1. WHERE THE FISH ARE

In major Western streams, fish are generally found in the upper fifth (surface) and lower fifth (bottom) because this is where they prefer to feed. There is not much action in the middle three-fifths of streams averaging five feet or more. A fisherman should concentrate on the two favorite dining rooms—surface and bottom—to get clues about where the fish are and how they are behaving.

2. HIGH WATER

Water conditions have a direct effect on fishing. In high water, the streams muddy up as they cut into dirt, sand, gravel, and debris. This often gives them a color ranging from creamed coffee to rich chocolate. When the water is swift it is called "roily."

High, fast water makes worms a good choice for bait because the wrigglers are washed into the current as the water cuts into banks. The fish will be looking for them, or for any other natural food that might be washed out of dirt crumbling away from a bank.

During high water, good results are obtained with short leaders and heavier-than-usual sinkers. The lead weight gets the bait down to the bottom through the currents, and the short leader is easier to handle and guide than a long one.

There is little need for the deceptive tactics a fisherman uses in clear, gentler waters. The turbulence and color of the roily stream conceals the line and short leader rather well. Also, the fish's main pre-occupation at such times is not so much fear as lying behind protective cover and waiting for what looks like food to pass by.

The fisherman's main job in fast water, then, is to get his bait to the fish quickly. The best thing to do is place it practically in front of a trout's nose so he can't miss seeing it. This may take repeated casts and some luck but it is the hard-working way of getting results.

In low water the primary objective is to use deception to get bait close enough for a fish to notice it.

In high water the primary objective of an angler is to place the bait or lure in front of a fish's nose.

3. LOW WATER

Later in summer, when the water run-off from snow packs and rain-swept mountains ends and the same stream is reduced to a milder stretch of water, the angler changes his tactics.

Long, fine leaders replace the short ones and caution replaces boldness when casting into riffles, the edges of undercut banks, and pools.

Now the springtime potholes, formerly filled with roaring water, have changed into peaceful pools fed by gentler currents. And fish living there can easily watch the landscape for suspicious movements of preying animals or humans.

Although summer waters in some locations can become murky due to rains, there is still the summer requirement for light tackle because fish automatically become spooky and wary in the season of low water.

4. TEMPERATURES

A fisherman should always note temperature conditions both in and out of the water.

Temperatures affect the behavior of a fish because as a cold-blooded animal he feels the cold or warmth of his surroundings from head to tail. He will seek a temperature which is most comfortable to his body and will rise to the surface or swim deep to find it. Therefore, the temperature often gives a good clue about how deep the fish lie.

Temperatures also give information about the possibility of insect hatches. A warm spell can speed up the hatching of larvae, for example, and when this happens it will bring fish to the surface to eat the flies.

Temperatures also suggest the kind of clothes a fisherman wears. This may not seem important, but it is. An uncomfortable fisherman is frequently a person who gives up quickly.

5. EDGES OF FAST WATER

A fast current is almost always bordered by waters which bubble and bounce, giving the impression that they are trying to halt the stream's swift flow. Under this bubbling condition the current builds a concentration of oxygen and food particles, a double-barrel feature which makes a nice dining room for fish. In such conditions, a trout or smallmouth bass likes to lie behind a protective rock or log, taking in oxygen that makes him feel frisky, and darting into the fast water for food, then back into the slower edge for a rest.

Many fishermen refer to fish feeding in this manner as being in a playful mood. Apparently fish like the exercise and excitement of bucking the fast current and then returning from it.

Two things fish like most are oxygen and food. Both may be abundant along the edges of fast water.

Anglers fishing such waters make casts upstream, letting their lures float in the current as naturally as possible so as to entice the fish to dart into the current and strike at them.

6. OBSTRUCTIONS

Obstructions in a stream create certain hot spots a fisherman should look for when examining a stretch of water. These often should be located before casting. Behind a rock or log there is often a slick eddy which provides a fish excellent shelter and a place to grab passing food.

In fast water, where the current flows rapidly within a few inches of the obstruction and seems too swift for a fish's comfort, a trout may lie close to it so the current can flow unimpeded over his slick body. This is called "lying tight" and under such conditions a fisherman tries to drop his lure in front of the fish's nose because the latter is undoubtedly looking straight ahead.

7. ALONG AN UNDERCUT BANK

Frequently there is a pool of water beneath a bank in the curve of a stream. Here, large trout lie close to

Gamefish are extremely streamlined. They can find shelter behind obstructions hard for a fisherman to see.

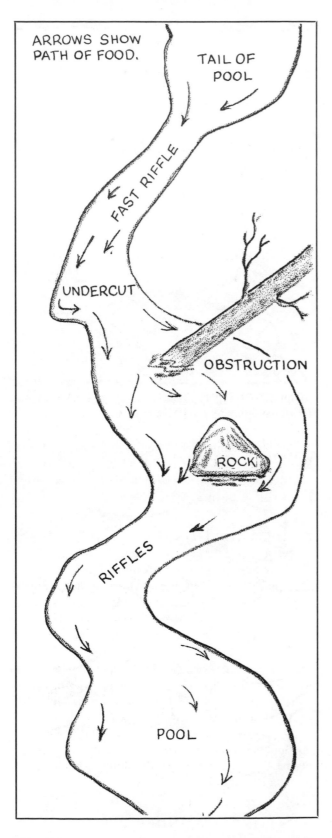

ARROWS SHOW PATH OF FOOD.

TAIL OF POOL

FAST RIFFLE

UNDERCUT

OBSTRUCTION

ROCK

RIFFLES

POOL

Many Western streams have a steeper runoff than their counterparts in other areas of the country. This steepness can create a wide variety of water in a short stretch.

shore in the protected spot, waiting for the food to pass by. It is not uncommon for a fisherman to fail to see such a hideaway because it is often hidden by grass or brush, or it is across the stream and inaccessible.

Trout in these quiet, protected locations don't like to leave their homes in daytime. Therefore, they must be fished at the depth or in the current in which they lie. This is usually done by presenting a deep bait in a way that allows it to float into the hole naturally and quietly.

8. FAST WATER SPLIT BY A ROCK

Rainbows love fast water and frequently take position ahead of a submerged rock where the current splits to either side of it. Brown trout will also lie in front, but not in as fast water as Rainbows enjoy. Brooks will take up position behind the rock.

If a fisherman is familiar with the species of fish contained in the stream, he will try to present his lures the way each member likes them best. And this local knowledge about the dominant species of fish is why some fishermen quickly fill their creels while others don't.

9. PROJECTIONS FROM A BANK

Sandspits, gravel piles, shoreline rocks, and logs create interesting eddies. As the water fights to get around the projections it often does so with such force that the current reverses itself. This condition can cause a fish to lie in the eddies of a pool facing downstream. Fishermen must remember this phenomenon when approaching a whirling eddy from downstream, or they may be seen by the fish.

10. POOLS

Pools have fast water at the head, a quiet middle section, and a shallow, smooth tail. Bigger fish take over a deep pool for shelter during daylight hours and force smaller fish into the riffles at the head of the pool. Minnows generally occupy the tail.

In the evening and sometimes in early morning, when the danger of marauding birds, animals, and daytime fishermen disappears, the larger fish often move into the shallower tail waters to seek food.

During the daytime, the best place to get action is to fish for the smaller 8 to 12-inch fish from the head of the pool. The big ones on the bottom may be encouraged to take bait or attack a slow-moving lure retrieved across the bottom. In the evening, the action is good on all sides of the pool.

11. CURRENTS

Trout will lie in current which flows to a speed of up to 50 feet per minute. In faster water they must swim to keep their position. The big fish like a spot where they can lie quietly in a comfortable area and have their food brought to them by the current.

When rock bottom measures 2-inch rock size and smaller, the current of a stream will have the same approximate speed from surface to bottom as it flows over the rocks.

Currents flowing over 12-inch and larger rocks have slower currents on the bottom than at the top because eddies are created by stones slowing the current. This can create a crisscrossing of underwater currents and cause drifting objects such as food, debris, or lures to act in an erratic way.

It is hard for a fisherman to see how the current in a boulder-strewn stream behaves. However, he must take the current's behavior into consideration because it has a vital effect on the way his leader and bait perform. It is one of the primary reasons why some fishermen can cast and hook fish while others who think they are fishing in the same way get nothing.

The "lucky" angler has learned the secret about the underwater currents and works his lures to take advantage of it. The "unlucky" ones don't even get a bite because they present their lures unnaturally.

12. RIFFLES

Fishermen who like to use a moving bait such as a fly or salmon egg with a lightweight sinker look for riffles to three feet deep where rocks on the bottom measure 12 inches and larger. They do this because they know from experience that these rocks offer many protective pockets where fish can lie and grab passing food.

Large rocks form eddies and slow the bottom current to a greater degree than that of the surface. A good fisherman should work his lures accordingly by casting upstream and allowing his bait, fly, or spinner to sink among the rocks and float in the eddies. He retrieves just fast enough to prevent too many snags.

If he casts across or downstream he should probably use a sinker to get his bait down. If he uses a fly the line should be of the sinking variety and the leader should be treated so it will sink also.

GRAVEL BOTTOM GIVES AN EVEN FLOW OF CURRENT.

BOULDERS ON BOTTOM GIVE UNEVEN FLOW OF CURRENT.

The sizes of rocks on a stream's bottom have much to do with the speeds and directions of the currents.

Riffles are favorite places to fish. Trout especially like them for shelter, oxygen, and food.

Fishing Western Lakes

If a fisherman hopes to catch fish consistently in a lake the first thing he should do is start learning about the lake he is going to fish. Otherwise he may join the many anglers who were disappointed before him and who probably decided the only sure place to find a fish is on a plate in a restaurant near the lake.

From the point of view of fish, there are a number of different types of lake waters in the West. And if the fish find them different, so should the fisherman.

One difference is between food resources in natural and man-made lakes, and their effect on the growth of fish. Another is the matter of warm or cold water; the former suits bass and the latter suits trout. A third difference is the presence or absence of tributary streams, an important factor in spawning and fish propagation because most trout do not multiply in lakes without tributary streams. Notable exceptions are brook and lake trout. A fourth is weather. Where top sport was produced one season, a rough winter may decimate the fish population and make the following season a poor one in any shallow lake.

These and other factors directly affect the kind of fish which inhabit a particular lake, and they also affect the way a man goes about trying to catch whatever fish might be in that lake. To combat these problems, this chapter tries to arm the angler with the kind of information which can give him a better chance of getting to a productive lake at the right time to do the right thing.

Lake waters differ

The natural lakes in Western mountains are old and established. Many support food supplies in stable water temperatures, so the native fish population is fairly constant. Some lakes, however, need restocking from time to time because of winter kills or some other reason. Some lakes are just plain barren.

Fishing natural lakes is done in the traditional ways. The major problem with most of these lakes is getting there. High-country lakes usually require well-planned pack trips.

Artificial lakes make a different picture. They have been built to take care of the burgeoning water needs of the West's exploding population. Thousands of new reservoirs have been built within the past few years. In these waters, with shorelines ranging from one to 1,000 miles, the fisherman may not have the same kind of luck with the lore and lures he uses successfully in the natural, established lakes where fish are adapted to their habitat.

The West's reservoir program is creating new kinds of water and accompanying fish habitats in mountains, valleys, foothills, and deserts, where no waters of consequence existed before. These waters are offering new challenges to fish management experts, whose business it is to raise healthy and catchable game-fish, and new challenges to fishermen, who must

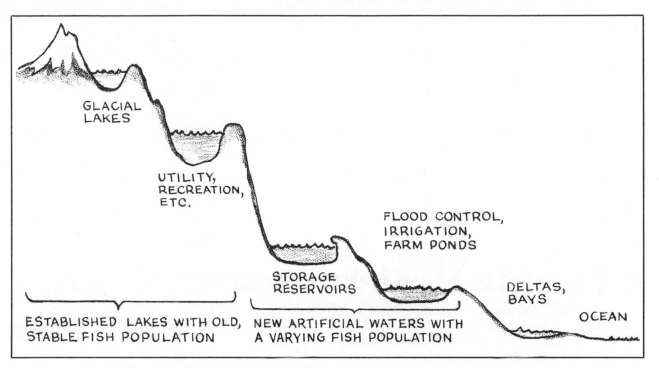

Western lakes range from two miles above sea level to more than a hundred feet below. Altitude is only one of several factors affecting the kind of fishing found.

learn how these fish are learning to behave in strange surroundings.

STOCKING NEW WATERS

Nearly all the new, man-made lakes and their connecting waterways are stocked with some species of gamefish. The exceptions are certain irrigation and flood control waters which have such a fluctuating water level that stocking them is not considered economically feasible. Fish die during the dry summer.

Soil formations, chemicals in the ground, climate, and paths of water runoff vary a great deal from one man-made lake building project to the next. A study must be made of each new artificial body of water before gamefish are planted. These studies can be involved and time-consuming, because the West has an inexhaustible variety of land areas, each with a different set of plant and fish growth problems. For example, unexpected salt deposits in the ground may create a salinity fatal to planted trout. Or another area may refuse to grow plants bass need to survive. All these problems have to be worked out. Sometimes it takes years to make the right set of choices.

ACTION IN A NEW LAKE

When a new area is flooded, the ground and surrounding vegetation generally are rich. This causes a natural water fertility, and fishing can almost always be rated from good to superior for several years.

After four or five years, fishing activity drops. As water flows in and out of the lake to be used for drinking, power, or some other purpose, the richness of the soil and plants gradually washes away and the waters become diluted or even sterile. This automatically reduces the production of food for fish to eat. As a consequence, fish start fighting for their existence. The competition for food prevents their prospering. Eventually they are driven to cannibalism.

The major problem for fish management scientists is to conquer local conditions, to find ways to enrich waters and stock them with the species of gamefish that will thrive in whatever conditions prevail.

NEW LAKE SPECIES

One solution which often works is to introduce a radically new species of fish. The selection of such a new species is frequently startling to fishermen. Instead of finding the expected trout or bass in still waters, they may discover saltwater fish taking their bait.

Examples of saltwater fish now being planted in interior lakes are striped bass, which thrive in both fresh and salt water; corvina, a cousin of the white bass; and sargo, a member of the grunt family. In tepid, inland lake waters planted striped bass are doing well. In dry, saline basins such as the Salton

Sea, fishermen are now enjoying good action from corvina and sargo.

Other examples of fish transplanted to new areas are the kamloops rainbow trout, which have prospered after being taken from Idaho lakes into waters of other states, and the splake, which is a Colorado cross between a female lake trout and a male brook trout. It does well in many coldwater lakes.

COLD OR WARM WATER?

There are three types of lakes: 1) coldwater lakes, which support trout; 2) cold-warmwater lakes, which support trout, bass, and sunfish; and 3) warmwater lakes, which support bass and sunfish. Where there are connecting streams between lakes, they will contain the same species of fish as the lakes do.

Coldwater lakes have a year-around coolness. They seldom rise above 65 degrees Fahrenheit. These lakes support trout and are found in mountains or wherever they can be fed by clear, cold streams and springs.

Cold-warmwater lakes get their name because they combine cold and warm water. They are generally large and deep. The deep part is cool enough to support trout even in summer, and the shallows are warm enough for bass or sunfish.

The water in warmwater lakes is too warm for trout. These lakes are often shallow, and have a lush underwater plant life that bass and sunfish like.

RESERVOIR FISHING

Reservoirs are built to store good, cool drinking water for a community, so the water temperature is generally suitable for trout.

These lakes have a high water level in spring and are low in fall. Carefully managed to prevent pollution, their use by fishermen is, where permitted at all, a privilege extended by local citizens through the reservoirs' water company management.

No community can afford acts or abuses which might interfere with its local water supply. Therefore, it is customary for fishermen to contact the local water company office for information related to fishing hours, registration, permission to use boats, and areas open to fishing in any such reservoir.

FISHING BEHIND POWER DAMS

The West's growing need for electric power has been the major reason for damming many of its large

Coldwater lakes are deep. Their waters seldom get warmer than 65°. Most are found at high elevations.

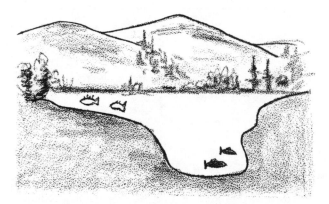

Cold-warmwater lakes combine deep pockets of cold water with shallow shelves of warm water.

Warmwater lakes are usually shallow and are found in warm to hot summer climates. Many are artificial.

streams. Some old-timers complain, but fishermen have profited from the program on many occasions. These reservoirs have high waters in spring, with a controlled runoff through summer and fall to manufacture power. During this time the water level is lowered. Attempts are made to keep this lowering within limits that will not harm fish. Unhappily, the attempts are not always successful, especially when the release is so erratic that a stream flows far below or far above its normal rate.

A major problem for designers and construction men is to design and build a dam that won't completely interfere with migratory fish such as salmon or steelhead as they travel up and down a stream while spawning. The fish migration problem has been attacked by the artificial means of a fish ladder, a special waterway fish can use to swim around the dam and into the lake behind it.

Another method is to create small fish hatcheries where artificial hatching and planting are used to offset the losses created by dams or diverted water.

FISHING FLOOD CONTROL LAKES

Flood control reservoirs are lakes which have been built to collect water to help stop floods. They are usually built in dry, arid country where the water runoff from heavy rains can cause flash floods and heavy damage.

Although flood control waters look pretty in spring when the grass is green and the wildflowers are at their prettiest, they are not good fishing waters. Since they dry up quickly in the dry season it is impractical to keep them well stocked with fish. Adequate minimum pool depths can be established in some cases, but these are very few.

FISHING IRRIGATION LAKES

During winter rains and snows the West stores water for farm use during the dry seasons of summer and fall. Water is collected in basins ranging in size from a tiny pond near a farmer's house to many-mile-long lakes built either privately or by the government.

The major problem in storing water for irrigation is that frequently the ponds or lakes are drawn to their bottoms during the dry season. This leaves a muddy, caked mess that is no good for boating, bathing, or fishing—and means death to the food supply for any fish that might survive in the holes.

Not all irrigation lakes fit this unfortunate category. Some of them, such as Big Bear Lake in the mountains

northeast of Los Angeles, are year-around outdoor paradises. But it is not uncommon in the West to see lakes in summer so low that their shores are 25 to 75 feet lower than their winter levels. This border of soil is incapable of enriching itself to produce the kind of water organisms on which fish could feed after winter waters again cover the barren area. This helps reduce fish life in the lake.

It is the hope of many sportsmen that a standard method of establishing minimum lake depths and provisions for fish forage can become fact, in compliance with the intent of the 1958 Congressional Fish and Wildlife Act. A meeting of the minds between developers, farmers, and outdoorsmen about maintaining lake water minimums would provide an improved combination of irrigation and recreation waters for the future.

FISHING RECREATION LAKES

In some areas where the scheme for conserving water has provided an abundance of it that surpasses the current needs of power or agriculture, lakes have been built for recreational purposes only. It is argued that this storage of water is like putting money in the bank for future need. In the meantime, the recreation factor is interest on the investment.

SMALL PONDS

Small ponds on farms and estates are great producers of bass and sunfishes. These small waters are stocked with gamefish to help keep them clean and free of mosquitoes.

Not infrequently, a fertile pond's water becomes overcrowded with fish and needs thinning. In such cases many farmers welcome a competent angler-sportsman who will help reduce the fish population with hook and line.

A fisherman likes the deal because he has a place where he can have fun, not only for himself, but also a place where he can take his children or grandchildren for the kind of action he wants them to have when they are learning to fish.

In many cases it is difficult for a city man to meet a farmer who will let him fish in a good pond. But getting acquainted with such a man doesn't take much more time or effort than trying to catch a limit of fish in a strange lake some distance away. And there is less chance of an empty creel.

FOUR IMPORTANT TIPS

1. An angler should first choose the lake areas in which he is primarily interested in fishing.

If a man knows where he is going, and why, he will have a more enjoyable and relaxing outing than if he is strange to the country. Also, as he develops more knowledge about local conditions he will bring in more catches.

2. He should contact people such as local Fish and Game Department personnel, Chambers of Commerce, and other appropriate agencies or sporting goods stores in the area concerned. These people are in the business of helping visitors, and when properly approached they can be gold mines of information.

3. The angler should be patient. The man-made lake program in the West is new. Depending upon location, these reservoirs have a wide variety of waters—alkaline, mineral, muddy, murky, clear, cold, tepid, or warm. They have a variety of fishing problems which cannot be solved overnight. The angler's main job is to find a lake where the waters support good fishing, and to concentrate his efforts there.

4. The desires of fishermen are often in competition with the desires of electric powermen, farmers, water suppliers, shipping, and industry.

An excellent thing for an angler to do is to work diligently and patiently for better fishing, and to get along with those whose cooperation can help him to get that better fishing.

HOW TO FIND FISH

In such a variety of waters as the thousands of lakes in the West—natural and man-made, big and little, deep and shallow, high and low altitude—there would seem to be no simple answer to the question, "Is there any general approach that will catch trout from the shore of any promising lake?"

Surprisingly, the answer is, "Yes. If there are trout in the lake, trout that feel like biting; if the fisherman follows the methods outlined in this chapter, and has a little luck, he should get results more often than not."

Making this broad, affirmative statement may sound like advertising, but there is no magic formula or gimmick in the prescription—and it does not include buying out a tackle store or hiring an expert for lessons or a guide to reach remote country.

In essence, this chapter is a summary compilation of thousands of scraps of evidence about what a

trout living in a lake likes or dislikes, where he spends his time, and, therefore, how, when, and where he bites.

TIME OF DAY

The time of day a fisherman chooses to try his luck in a lake is important. Except in early spring and late fall, a typical lake fish does not like to expose himself to the bright sunlight near a lake's surface.

When he does swim near the surface he is more comfortable in the gray light of morning or evening. This is especially true from June through September when old Sol is directly overhead and working at his brightest and hottest. There are several good reasons for this.

Summer sunshine heats the water's surface. When the surface gets too warm for comfort fish swim into deeper and cooler water where life is more enjoyable.

Fish are afraid of bright sunshine because it makes them more visible. And since fish must be constantly wary of their natural enemies—animals, birds, other fish—they lurk in dark places during midday to keep out of danger. Their philosophy is to see but not be seen.

Fish in a lake dislike bright sunshine, especially in the summer months from mid-June through September.

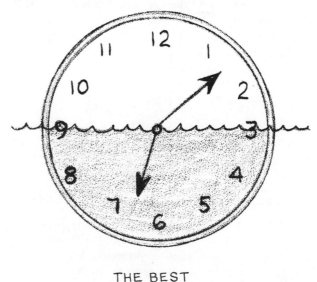

THE POOREST
FISHING TIMES

THE BEST
FISHING TIMES

Sunlight makes strange and suspicious shadows. Fish don't like weird shadows and who can blame them? Weird shadows scare human beings too.

In the evening, when the sun has left the surface of the lake and the water begins to cool, trout visit the shallows to forage for food.

There are in general two best times for fishing— morning and evening. In morning, the fish start feeding after a night's rest and the sunshine isn't yet bright enough to bother them.

This doesn't mean it is impossible to catch fish in a lake at midday—far from it. Fish are catchable at all hours; but during the warm, sunny part of any day a fisherman needs more skill, perhaps a wider variety of tackle, and more luck to get results from shoreline fishing than he does in morning and evening when conditions are favorable.

LAKE CONTOUR

One of the most important tasks for the lake fisherman is the locating of offshore ledges or drop-offs around the lake's rim.

These ledges are popular hatching places for underwater life such as crustaceans (shrimp) or water larvae (insects). Where such food resources exist there will also be fish eating them. So a ledge is an excellent place to start fishing.

Generally, on the lee or protected side of the lake or an obstruction, small fish frequent the ledge area to wait for food to be blown into the water from the land. On the windward side of the lake or an obstruction, large fish lie in the ledge areas waiting for food to float or be blown to them from across the lake.

The primary ledge around a lake is in many cases within easy casting distance. It is often found from 10 to 30 feet from the shoreline at depths of 5 to 25 feet.

Sometimes a map is available which a fisherman can study to locate primary ledges and identifying landmarks. Occasionally it can be spotted by looking down on the lake from a high elevation. Not infrequently it takes only good old "horse sense" to figure where the ledge lies.

In any case, it is important to find because the primary ledge area is the best place for a shore fisherman to start hunting for fish in a strange lake. Fish will be there.

The rims and ridges of a lake basin support plant and small animal life in a lake, and affect the movement of water in a lake, so fish visit them frequently.

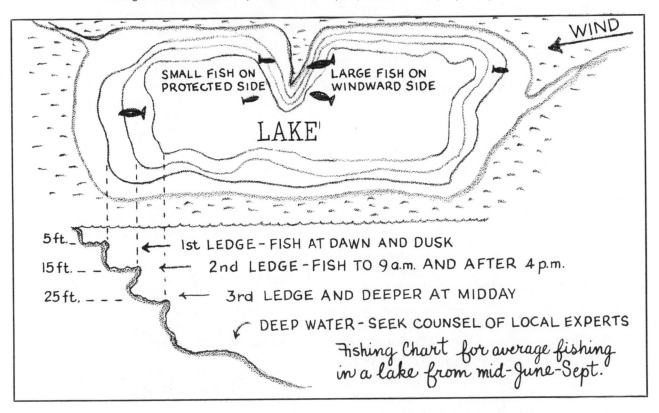

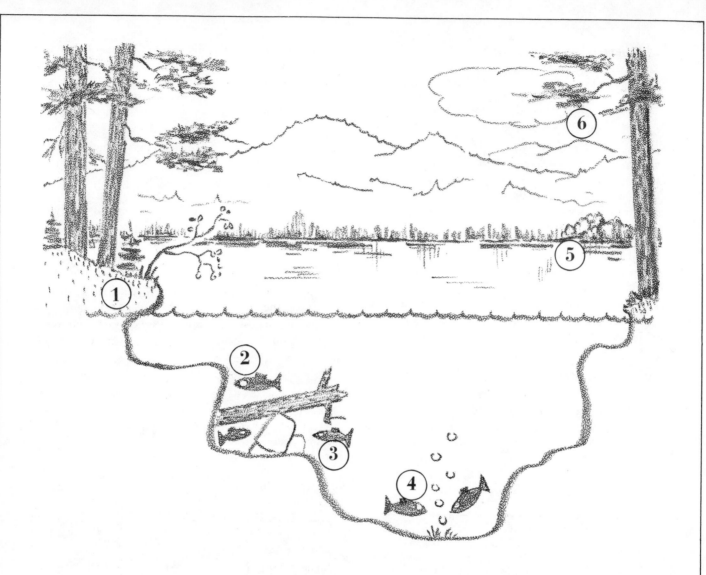

Six-way check list for lake anglers

Successful lake fishermen study one lake thoroughly; they don't scatter their efforts too widely. Also, they use the low-water season in fall to find below-the-surface information that can't be seen in spring. These are points to seek.

1. Plant growth. Examine plant growth along the shoreline in and out of the water. This gives clues to the location of underwater weed beds fish may frequent to find food.

2. Contour. Study the lake's contour to discover likely locations of underwater ledges. Here is where fish frequently lurk when hiding or resting in comfortable water.

3. Submerged cover. Look for submerged rocks and logs which provide fish with protective cover and comfortable shelter.

4. Springs. Try to find out if and where there are underwater springs in the lake. These are favorite places for fish seeking the kind of oxygenated, exhilarating waters which make them feel good.

5. Inlets and outlets. Study a map or walk the shoreline of the lake to locate inlets and outlets. Food is often more plentiful in these areas and where there is food there should be fish.

6. Winds. Study the direction of prevailing winds. Find a spot where good casts can be made with a cross or carrying wind to an area where the surface is rippled. A slightly choppy surface helps hide the fishing rig from the fish's eyesight.

P.S. Seventh, locate a comfortable spot to lie down and dream while the fish "ain't biting."

44

Limnology

Every fisherman should know something about the way water temperatures affect the behavior of fish because an understanding of the subject gives a man important clues about where to fish.

The study of water temperatures is a major part of limnology, science devoted to a specialized study of freshwater lakes and ponds. It applies especially to the biological, chemical, and physical conditions of the waters in which fish live.

High in interest to fishermen are the limnological theories related to the effects of water temperatures on the eating habits of gamefish such as trout and bass.

PUTTING LIMNOLOGY TO WORK

Water on the surface of a lake takes heat from (or gives heat to) the air, depending on the season and time of day. Therefore, a year-around working relationship of taking and giving exists between surface water and atmosphere.

Second, as water gets colder it gets heavier until it reaches its maximum weight at 39.2° (4° Centigrade).

To say it another way, as water temperatures go above or below 39.2° the water becomes lighter.

So, as the water temperatures in the seemingly quiet body of a lake change there is a constant up-and-down movement due to the rise and fall of lighter and heavier water. It may be almost nil, gradual, or sudden, depending upon the expanse and depth of water, the heat from the sun, air temperatures at night, winds, or underwater springs, but there is always some movement.

If a fisherman understands these changing water conditions and he also knows the favored water temperature for a particular kind of fish he will have a better chance of making a catch, because, according to limnological theory, an angler using a thermometer and depth readings can scientifically locate waters where fish should be and concentrate his efforts there.

FEEDING ACCORDING TO TEMPERATURES

Many experiments have been made in hatcheries and controlled streams to study the feeding habits of fish under various water temperature conditions.

It has been found, for example, that an average rainbow trout in 45° water takes approximately two days to digest and dispose of a small amount of food. Only 5 degrees higher at 50°, the same fish digests its food every 24 hours. At 55 to 60° he can digest it within 12 hours and so within this bracket he is at his ravenous best.

Therefore, speaking statistically, a fisherman has four to six times more chances of getting a rainbow "to bite" where the water temperature is 55 to 60° than he has where the water is a cold 45°.

WINTER HIBERNATION PERIOD

In winter the heaviest water at 39.2° is on the lake's bottom and the lightest water is at the top, just beneath the ice, at a temperature close to 32°. In between the bottom and the top will be varying water temperatures, depending upon the lake.

During winter, fish will be relatively inactive because at water temperatures of 45° or below (see chart) trout take two days or more to digest the little food they eat.

At this time of year they seek the warmest water in which they can find oxygen and food. In murky or deep lakes, they may choose a spot near the surface in waters that are too cool for comfort because they want to be near oxygen produced in daylight. This is because an absence of light below the water's surface slows down the photosynthesis process of vegetation, which produces oxygen to absorb carbon dioxide. Since a lack of oxygen hinders breathing, fish will choose to exist in water that is too cold for comfort if they can find oxygen in it. They will also live in water that is too warm for comfort if it contains the oxygen they need.

Perhaps it is well to mention here that trout require more oxygen than some other kinds of fish, and one reason they prefer cold water is because it is capable of holding more oxygen than warm water. Spiny-ray fish, such as bass, require less oxygen, and so can live in warm water.

SPRING TURNOVER

At springtime a pronounced physical change takes place that vastly improves fishing.

As the sun warms the lake's icy surface the surface temperature rises to the maximum density figure of 39.2°. Since this is water at its heaviest, it begins to sink toward the bottom. As it does, it mixes with or

WATER TEMPERATURES AFFECT FEEDING HABITS OF GAMEFISH

FEEDING ACTIVITY OF A RAINBOW TROUT IN DIFFERENT WATER TEMPERATURES

The chart's temperatures are necessarily approximate because a native rainbow in Washington may be most active in 55° water whereas a California rainbow may favor water of 60°. The general pattern of the feeding curve is accurate, however.

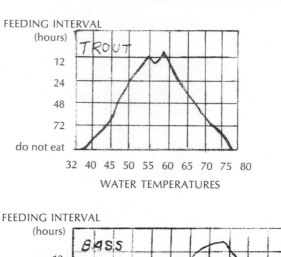

FEEDING INTERVAL
(hours)

12
24
48
72
do not eat

32 40 45 50 55 60 65 70 75 80
WATER TEMPERATURES

FEEDING ACTIVITY OF A LARGEMOUTH BASS IN DIFFERENT WATER TEMPERATURES

Bass thrive in warmer water than trout. In warm lake waters of Southern California and Arizona, they reach spawning maturity in one year. In colder waters of Idaho or Washington, they may take three years to reach maturity.

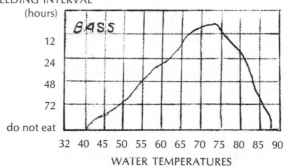

FEEDING INTERVAL
(hours)

12
24
48
72
do not eat

32 40 45 50 55 60 65 70 75 80 85 90
WATER TEMPERATURES

SEASONAL BEHAVIOR OF LAKES WITH FOUR SEASONS

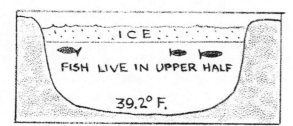

LAKE IN WINTER. The ice at 32° is aerated and light in weight, so it floats. Heaviest water, at 39.2° lies on the bottom. In between are waters of different temperatures. Fish choose a level with good oxygen supply for winter hibernation.

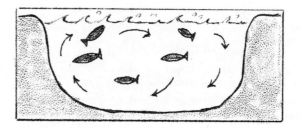

SPRING TURNOVER. The sun heats icy surface waters. As top layer reaches 39.2° it begins to sink. This pushes other water up. Soon a large body of water is rotating like a wheel. Fish are everywhere, especially at surface, to get oxygen.

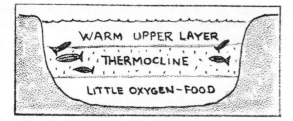

SUMMER DOLDRUM. As surface waters get warm, they get lighter and stay on top. Cold water rests at the bottom. Between the two is a cushion called the thermocline. This is where most fish stay, for oxygen, food, temperature.

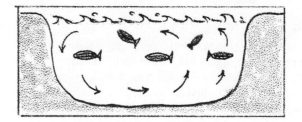

AUTUMN TURNOVER. Fall weather cools the surface. This causes water to become heavier, and it sinks, pushing warmer water up. The weather continues to cool new surface water. Finally, a portion reaches 39.2°, and it settles to the bottom.

displaces waters of other temperatures. This phenomenon automatically starts a turnover of the lake's waters.

As winds and sunshine add oxygen to the water as well as encourage its turnover, fish begin swimming to the surface to gulp the fresh stuff. After the oxygen exhilarates them, and the temperatures rise to their liking, they begin to eat heartily.

At this thawing period, the angler at a mountain lake enjoys great action—thrilling action—as the hungry trout rise to fill their stomachs after a long winter's nap.

The first fish to hit will be the lake trout because they thrive in colder waters than other trout species, and so rise to the surface before others. Up from the bottom they will come, and they are soon found swimming and carrying on at all water depths including the surface. About a week later they will be followed by other trout such as brook and rainbow.

Surface lures work especially well at this time, particularly along the banks and in windward areas where the winds deposit food and the rippling water provides tasty oxygen.

This seasonal paradise for a fisherman lasts only a week or two before settling down to a more normal activity.

SUMMER DOLDRUM PERIOD

As the summer sun warms the lake, it causes the surface water to become lighter in weight than the water underneath. This creates a fairly static condition with relatively little vertical motion of lake water except the morning action of the surface, which may cool sufficiently during the night to create slight down currents by dawn.

This condition remains the same throughout the summer until the reverse process of spring turnover starts in fall.

During summer, in lakes of 50-foot depth and more, three temperature layers are established: Warm water at the surface, cold water on the bottom, and in between a cushion layer, known technically as the "thermocline."

The surface waters of lakes beneath a warm summer sun are generally barren of gamefish because they are too warm, except perhaps in evening and morning. Neither do the fish like the deep, cool bottom of a large lake because there may be a lack of oxygen and food down there. Sunlight cannot penetrate the depths to foster photosynthesis.

A fish will choose the cushion layer, or "thermocline," as his summer home. This is the area a fisherman should try to find if he hopes to have some good lake fishing in summer. And when he does find it, he will have more luck at the thermocline's top level, or just above it, than he will beneath it.

There are two ways of finding the thermocline area:

1. One is the scientific method of using a thermometer to test water temperatures at various depths. Most experts using this technique test lake waters at 10-foot depth intervals and continue their readings until they find the temperature indicating the thermocline layer which usually supports the fish they seek. Then they measure the length of line with which they lowered the thermometer to find the promising temperature, and this gives them the depth to start fishing.

2. The other method is the "educated-guess" system. Here a guess is made based upon the size of the lake and the assumption that nearly all thermoclines are found between 30 and 60 feet deep, depending upon the lake's depth and surface. Wind action should also be considered, because wind can keep a lake surface in turmoil to drive the thermocline deeper. Lakes with little wind have a thermocline nearer the surface.

Upon finding what seem to be promising temperature readings, the depth is checked and then a study is made of the lake's contour. It is important that identifying landmarks be noted. (See the section, "Fishing from a boat.")

TROUT IN SHALLOW LAKES

In lakes not deep enough to support a thermocline layer fishermen can be sure that native fish have found a substitute for it.

Generally, when shallow lakes have a warm summer surface yet support cold water fish such as trout, there are some cooling conditions which take the place of the thermocline.

1. Underwater springs create a cool and oxygen producing area where fish collect and live comfortably.

2. A deep bowl is someplace in the lake bottom where water stays cooler and native fish collect and live comfortably.

3. Tributary streams create underwater currents where fish find food and enjoy cooler waters.

It is the angler's job to find the underwater springs, deep bowl, or tributary streams. If he knows what he is looking for, it is easy.

FALL COMEBACK

In fall the colder nights start the reverse of the spring turnover process. As the cold air reduces the surface water temperature it gets heavier and sinks, pushing up lighter and warmer water to be cooled.

As this process continues the water turns over and reaches a colder and colder state. During this time, fish begin rising again and eating voraciously almost everywhere, including the surface.

Then as the surface water begins to freeze and the heavy 39.2° water settles to the bottom, the fish seek the most comfortable temperature containing adequate oxygen and food and settle in for a long winter.

The food cycle in lakes

In all good fishing waters there are invisible, free-floating organisms composed of plant and animal life. These microscopic creatures are called plankton. They are the basic food supply for fish life.

The plant form of plankton is made of many types of vegetable cells. The oily variety is called diatoms and scientists say that rich deposits of them deep in the earth have helped create the world's petroleum resources. The animal part of plankton is elementary cellular life, such as the transparent water flea, which feeds on the vegetable matter.

When organisms such as these are grouped in the water, the lump sum is called algae. As light reaches this substance, the process of photosynthesis takes place, and carbon dioxide is exchanged for oxygen. This helps create energy from the sun into food. The more sunshine that hits algae, the faster the process functions and the greener and less clear the water becomes.

Small fish and water insects live on both types of plankton, and thus grow large enough to become live food for trout and bass.

A gamefish can also feed directly off plankton by sucking water into his mouth, and then ejecting the water through his gills while the plankton remains to be swallowed.

It takes steady work and exercise to eat this way but some of the world's largest whales live entirely by the method. Therefore, although it is strenuous it still must be regarded as nourishing if the eater knows how to do it.

In most cases, however, 70% of a trout's or bass's diet is composed of water life higher up the development ladder than plankton.

These gamefish prefer to eat freshwater shrimp, water insects in hatched or unhatched stages, and small fish that are easy to catch.

PLANKTON IN ARTIFICIAL LAKES

A major problem in fish management today is to find a way to supply enough forage food such as plankton, insects, or tiny fishlife to feed gamefish planted in artificial lakes.

Due to water dilution or non-fertile surroundings many of the West's new reservoirs have insufficient minerals to enrich the lake bottom's soil content so as to encourage the growth of enough rich plankton and water life to take care of gamefish needs.

Another common problem to many reservoirs is having their water drained off, which exposes water plants to the air causing them to die. Later, when fall and winter rains arrive the waters are deposited in a relatively barren area. There will be an absence of chemicals and minerals which are so necessary to plant and animal growth.

Therefore, to solve problems such as poor soil, lack of plant life, and diluted waters, fish management must find new ways for supplying food to gamefish in many artificial lakes. Otherwise the number of fish will diminish as the amount of food diminishes.

The sale of fishing licenses will also drop in the same ratio and this can become a matter of great political concern to sportsmen's organizations and holders of elective offices having to do with water resources.

FORAGE FISH

A current program for speeding the production of food for gamefish in artificial lakes is to introduce new types of forage fish upon which the gamefish can feed.

One highly successful forage fish now being introduced into Western artificial lakes to help solve the food shortage is the threadfin shad.

An import from Tennessee, this little fish's main mission in life seems to be that of growing into a tasty mouthful for a trout or bass.

On meager food resources he multiplies rapidly, grows quickly to a maximum 5 to 6 inches and is not the kind of elusive swimmer a hungry gamefish must wear itself out trying to capture.

The threadfin's needs are few and he puts existing plankton to work so well that many biologists are

Almost all of the new artificial lakes in the West are beautiful, but they are often a problem for fish management. Many become sterile in three to five years.

now saying the little import has given them a sure way for providing trout and bass with what they need to eat.

FORAGE FISH AND FISHING

Fishermen should ask about the planting of forage fish, such as threadfin shad, in lakes they intend to fish. Local fish and game authorities can give this information.

For example, in California's Shasta Lake where threadfins have been introduced the trout are eating them voraciously. However, because threadfins roam over the entire lake the fishermen have had to change their technique.

Where once big trout were caught only near the shoreline or along ledges, now they are also found in the depths of the lake's middle because the little forage fish are there also. And where there is gamefish food there will be gamefish eating it.

A good technique for fishing a large lake planted with forage fish is to use a thermometer or make a guess to find the thermocline layer at which gamefish will be lying.

In mid-summer, for example, the thermocline depth in a large lake such as Shasta will be at 40 to 55 feet deep.

After establishing the depth he plans to fish, the angler then attaches a silver spoon, with perhaps a touch of red on it, to a 3-foot leader. Using a weighty sinker, which may or may not be attached to a sinker release device, the lure is let down so it will troll slowly at the 40 to 55-foot depth.

The object is to have the lure resemble a shiny, wobbling threadfin and experience has shown that a fisherman trolling at this depth can feel optimistic about hooking a five pounder.

If the fisherman prefers to troll a worm, streamer fly, spinner, or live bait instead of a spoon that is his business. However, the method is the same.

PLANTING FORAGE FISH

Under no circumstances should fishermen dump live bait, such as minnows, into a lake.

Many people make the sad mistake of thinking they are helping fish management when they toss a bucket of live minnows into a body of water.

On the contrary, such an act often introduces unwanted species of fish harmful to fishing, such as carp, suckers, miscellaneous scavenger fish, and eels. These are hardy fishes with feeding and propagation habits that quickly destroy the balance of vegetation and water life so necessary to gamefish prosperity.

Fishing can be ruined for years by one angler's careless or ignorant act. That is why many states have laws forbidding or restricting the use of live fish for bait. They don't want to encourage the risk of having fish pests take over the waters.

The planting of forage fish is a job for the proper authorities. It is their business. They know exactly what to do and what not to do.

The way for a fisherman to cooperate is to use artificial lures, worms, or eggs for bait and not live minnows or small fish which have not been captured in the lake being fished. This helps reduce the risk of polluting good waters with undesirable species of destructive fish.

It is a fisherman's responsibility to take care of fishing waters just as much as fish management's.

Shore fishing for trout

Perhaps the best all-around gear for keeping bait in the water from a lake's shoreline is spinning equipment. Both the open-face or closed-face model spinning reels are satisfactory.

With spinning equipment the occasional fisherman can keep his bait or lure working in the water a greater part of the time than with fly or plug casting equipment.

If a single spinning line is to be selected for trout fishing from the shore of a lake it should be a 4-pound test monofilament. A lighter weight line, such as 2-pound test, is so soft and flexible it requires more expert handling and a novice will have trouble keeping it unsnarled and working properly. A heavier line, such as 8-pound test, drags against the water to make give-away actions which scare trout in fairly clear water. However, it is a fine choice for bass.

As with the stream fisherman, an important but often neglected part of a lake shore angler's equipment is his terminal tackle—the leader, sinker, and hook which holds the bait.

For attachment to a 4-pound test spinning line a good terminal hookup is either a 7½-foot fly-line leader measuring 3X or 4X or about 4 to 5 feet of 2-pound test monofilament line. To this leader is attached a No. 12 size claw-type hook for use with salmon egg or a No. 8 hook for using a worm or shrimp.

The sinker should be just heavy enough for casting purposes. The best choice is a small buckshot fastened about 18 inches above the hook.

The light leader allows the bait to drift in the water naturally. The No. 12 hook is small enough to be completely covered by a single salmon egg but large enough to hook a trout firmly. The buckshot sinks the bait slowly and with little give-away action.

With a lightweight terminal rig of this type a fish may approach the bait without suspicion and when he nudges it, the egg or worm will behave in a natural manner.

This terminal rig is designed for use with the "count" method described below.

FINDING HUNGRY FISH

A lake fish must be on the move to bite. If he remains in one spot he is resting and not eating, unless he is feeding off the mouth of an inlet stream, which often happens after a storm. So after a fisherman studies his lake and decides upon the likely places his quarry

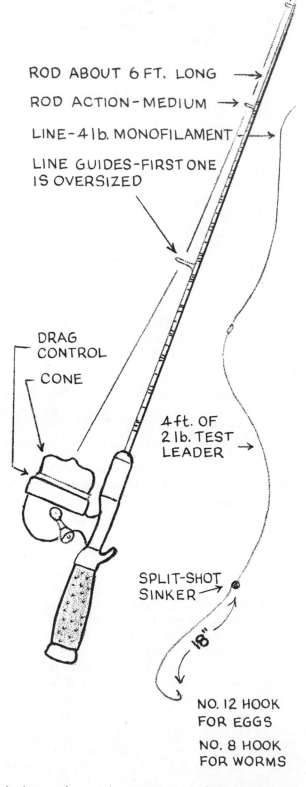

ROD ABOUT 6 FT. LONG →

ROD ACTION—MEDIUM →

LINE—4 lb. MONOFILAMENT →

LINE GUIDES—FIRST ONE IS OVERSIZED

DRAG CONTROL CONE

4 ft. OF 2 lb. TEST LEADER →

SPLIT-SHOT SINKER →

18"

NO. 12 HOOK FOR EGGS

NO. 8 HOOK FOR WORMS

Spinning equipment is easy to use, relatively inexpensive. This typical outfit is good for most fresh water.

COUNT OF 6

COUNT OF 9

COUNT OF 12

FISH FEEDING AT DEPTH COUNT OF 12

A good way to hunt for fish in a lake is to cast the same weight sinker and same length of line, but to vary the time lapse before starting to retrieve.

will visit while prowling for food he starts searching for his fish.

Lake fish are gregarious and generally move in schools. So in strange waters the angler's first job is to find the schools. He does this by making casts of assorted distances. Then he works his retrieves to vary the depth at which the bait floats in the water or moves across the bottom.

To get best results the angler should fish his bait slowly. Using his spinning rod and reel to cast his terminal rig of buckshot sinker and baited hook, he carefully notes the length of each cast and the depth at which he fishes.

For example, after a 40 foot cast he may count to 6 as he lets his bait sink before starting his retrieve. If he gets no action after a few 6 counts he may try some 9 or 12 counts to let the bait sink to a deeper level before retrieving. During this procedure he should not change his buckshot sinker because if he uses a heavier or lighter sinker he will naturally have to adjust his count to fit the faster or slower sinking caused by the change in the sinker weight.

In using this method the fisherman establishes a control for himself. By staying with one weight of sinker (buckshot) he always knows by his casting technique how much line he has out and by his count how deep the bait is when a fish strikes it.

When the fish-biting action starts he is ready to go to work because he knows exactly how far to cast and how deep to let his bait sink to reach the spot where he got a good bite. A major problem among many novices is that they feel a bite and then wonder what part of the lake it came from. The expert always knows.

WHEN FISH STRIKE WORK FAST

An expert angler hunting for fish is continually on the move. However, when he gets a strike he stops and fishes at the exact spot where he felt a fish.

He works the area hard because the chances are good that a school of feeders may be in the vicinity and he will be able to land several fish before the school swims to another area.

MANEUVERING THE BAIT

Fast fishing with frequent casts can also scare fish. Fishermen should remember that a lure must be in the water and not in the air or on the bank to catch fish.

Therefore, retrieves should be made slowly after each cast so as to keep the bait in the water as much as possible. Also, this technique provides more natural, tantalizing, and less frightening action—the kind that gets fish in ordinary circumstances.

To get the best results with bait the fisherman casts it to the water depth he thinks fish are working. Then he makes tiny tugs on the line to manipulate the bait, which can be either fresh such as a salmon egg or worm or artificial such as a plug or spinner.

The motions must be unhurried and it should be remembered that the movements are made to attract fish and not frighten them. The primary purpose is to persuade one of the members of a school of swimming fish to hit the bait before his pals can get to it.

If the bait is on the bottom the fisherman should give it an occasional tug to lift it and cause it to float a few seconds before it settles again. This brings the bait up and out of the mud or rocks of the bottom, an especially important thing to do when it rests in dark depths.

Occasionally, when a fisherman is sure fish are present but he gets no action with his bait he may attach a flashing spinner-blade attractor from 12 to 24 inches above the bait. The purpose is to call attention to the tasty piece of food that is trailing behind the flasher so a fish will take it.

Sometimes an angler about to leave an area that hasn't produced tries a couple of very fast retrieves. What usually scares fish may catch a non-conformist or two.

MANEUVERING THE ROD

After a fisherman makes his cast from shore he should keep his rod tip low. The reason is to reduce the effect of wind blowing against the line. A wind-blown line can cause the lure to act erratically. It also interferes with the feel of a fish's nibble.

After making his cast, the fisherman should hold a loop or two of line with his thumb and forefinger. This not only gives him line control but is also a method for giving the sensitive nerves of his finger tips an opportunity to feel the slightest nick from a fish mouthing or playing with the bait.

Holding a line in this manner provides a much more direct way of feeling a fish's nibble than relying upon the nibble to transmit itself down the line, rod, reel handle and hand.

Fish frequently mouth the bait to taste and test it before swallowing it. During this time an angler

should let the fish have freedom of movement with the bait. It is done by letting the loops of extra line slide through the finger tips. This deception gives the fish a feeling of safety as he moves the bait in his mouth and encourages him to take a firmer hold and then swallow it.

SETTING THE HOOK

Perhaps one of the least understood techniques in fishing is the correct movement of the rod to set the hook.

Invariably, when the novice fisherman feels a bite he excitedly raises his hand which holds the rod, in an effort to hook his fish. This is a mistake. Raising the rod butt up actually bends the rod in an arc to automatically put slack line between the rod tip and fish. See page 26 for the proper method.

A common mistake among shoreline fishermen is trying to set the hook too fast. Not only does a hurried movement jerk away the hook but it also frightens the fish which can cause them to scurry into deep water for safety.

When fish are wary, line is held gently with fingers. When a fish nibbles, let out line to encourage boldness.

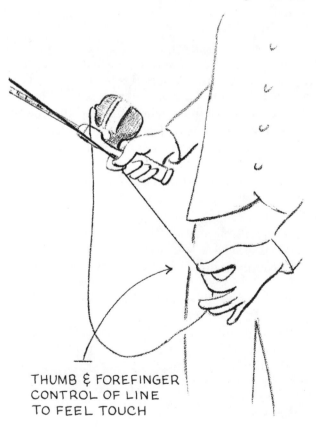

THUMB & FOREFINGER
CONTROL OF LINE
TO FEEL TOUCH

Four steps toward successful spin-fishing: 1) After casting, hold rod tip low. 2) When fish is on, don't bring him in too fast. Let him fight. 3) Play the fish until he flops over onto his side. 4) Beach a fish on the shore; net him from a boat.

BRINGING LAKE FISH TO SHORE

Before casting, a good spin fisherman will have his drag brake set properly. For 4-pound test line he sets it so he can feel the braking action, but so he does not have to tug sharply to get line off the spool.

When he hooks a fish, the fisherman holds his rod at approximately a 45° angle.

A low rod tip — say 25° — puts too much dependence on the tiny line and also on the brake. This may result in a broken line and a lost fish. A high rod tip — at about 70° — puts too much reliance on the spinning rod's action (a fly rod on the other hand is built exactly for this type action), and in this case too the fish might break away.

So, as the retrieve begins, the spinning rod is held at about a 45° angle. The size and fight of the fish then determines how much braking action the angler needs to bring in his catch. The hand holding the rod is next to the brake adjustment, and can make quick changes to meet conditions.

To avoid line twist, the reel crank should not be turned while the fish is taking out line. To slow the fish, pump him by raising then lowering the rod tip, and reeling in the slack line produced by this action.

The main objective is to let the fish know who is the boss. This is done by keeping a firm line between rod tip and fish. Then, by constant pressure and maneuvering, the angler steers the ever-tiring fish to the landing net or bank.

REMEMBER 4 POINTS

In summary, it is a good idea to remember 4 points.

1. Rig the terminal tackle properly.

2. Find a major ledge and fish it slowly.

3. Keep a taut line and always feel and watch its action so as to be ready to strike.

4. Fish bait slowly and stick to a plan of action.

Shorefishing for bass

The same fundamentals govern bass fishing from the shores of a lake as they do for trout.

The major exception is a change to slightly heavier tackle instead of a change in fishing technique.

Bass are sturdy fellows, especially in climates that provide the kind of year around warmth and food they like best. In such favorable areas the "bronzebacks" reach 5 pounds and over as compared to 1 and 2 pounds in cooler northern lakes.

Around bass waters a fisherman should be careful about voicing opinions concerning the relative merits of a bass vs. trout; many bass anglers are convinced that their favorite is the world's greatest battler. The truth of the matter lies in the place where the fish are caught—in warm waters bass will be at their fighting best and in cold waters the trout will have the edge.

A BASIC RIG FOR LARGEMOUTHS

There are many rigs suitable for largemouth bass fishing in a lake. These include fly, plug-casting, and spinning outfits with light to heavy-action rods, reels, lines, and lures. One of the determining factors is the kind of fishing to be done — surface, sub-surface, or deep.

An all-around outfit that will do a good job for anglers after largemouths and will withstand abuse is a spinning rig with closed-face reel.

ROD. For the average fisherman a medium-action, 6½ to 7-foot rod is recommended because it handles lightweight to medium-heavy lures satisfactorily, and is sturdy enough to drive home a hook in the bony jaw of a bass.

LINE. For bass fishing the line should be at least 8-pound test, and can be as heavy as 15-pound test. Lines of this size are light enough to cast well, but tough enough to be dragged through fouling weeds without breaking, to lose lures and fish.

REEL. The closed-face spinning reel makes up in sturdiness what it lacks in ability to cast lines long distances. In the weed-filled waters largemouths love, sturdiness makes it a good choice.

TERMINAL TACKLE. Swivels and/or a snap and swivel in No. 10 size are recommended at the end of the line. These rotating devices allow a lure to spin or wobble without twisting line. Also, the snap arrangement enables an angler to change lures quickly, an important advantage for a man after finicky bass.

In clear water, the swivel works better alone, and is installed between the line and about a 3-foot leader.

Much bass fishing is done with casts into quiet water where there are no currents or boat motion to help give the lure movement. Therefore, the angler must develop casting and retrieving skills that will fool fish.

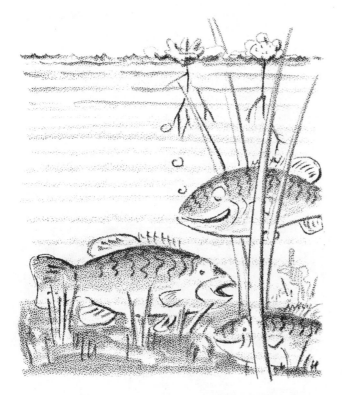

Largemouth bass prefer lakes and ponds where warm waters combine with soft bottom, underwater weed beds.

Smallmouth bass prefer clear, moving waters of low-altitude streams, or cool, clear lake waters.

In murky waters the bait or lure can be tied directly to the line, and hook size can range as large as No. 2. In clear waters, such as those covering gravel bottom areas where smallmouth bass flourish, a 4 lb. test leader about 3 feet long is advisable. The sinker for bait fishing should be just heavy enough for casting the line a fair distance. Hook size should be about No. 8.

The owner of a spinning outfit can quickly change from readiness for trout to bass by changing the line spool on his reel. All spinning fishermen should carry at least two spools of line—4 lb. test for trout and 8 to 10 lb. test for bass. For bait casting rods, 15 and 20 lb. test lines are favorites.

BASS BAITS

Bass have unpredictable and frustrating feeding habits. At times they eat ravenously such food as worms or grasshoppers. Then they may suddenly switch their attention to something as odd as cigarette butts or other peculiar objects floating on or near the surface. At this time an angler could throw a handful of worms at a bass and he may not touch them. Trout can be frustrating, but bass are the all-time champions at strange feeding habits.

A fisherman should be prepared for these unpredictable whims by having an assortment of spinners, plugs, and wobblers to use on the finicky creatures when they suddenly quit taking his bait. These may not get results either but the angler will have the satisfaction of knowing that he tried hard.

FINDING LARGEMOUTHS

Largemouth bass prefer quiet waters that cover a soft or mud bottom. They like water at least 10 degrees warmer than trout and they love the kind of protection offered by the shade of lily pads, reeds, underwater moss, and logs.

Often, the dark color of their environment may prevent their seeing a piece of bait attached to a hook and so artificial lures such as spinners, wobblers and plugs get good results.

FINDING SMALLMOUTHS

Smallmouth bass prefer fairly clear water on a gravel or rocky bottom, and they like to be near plant life from which they can dart in and out to seek food. The smallmouth fares better than largemouth bass in the cool, clear waters of northern lakes.

Fishing from a boat

If you can use a boat, it is usually the easiest way to fish a lake.

Many anglers prefer this method because they believe, and rightly so, that repeated casts from one spot along the shoreline make fish wary. It puts them down.

On the other hand, they argue, trolling has little adverse effect on fish. Actually, the steady noise of an outboard motor or rhythmic sound of oars may awaken fish and cause them to move around and start eating.

It is not uncommon for either salt or freshwater fishermen to report seeing a large fish swimming in the wake of a rotating propeller. This seems to indicate that curiosity is a stronger factor than fear insofar as fish and outboard motors are concerned. Also the turbulence created by the propeller adds to the water's oxygen content.

The boat fisherman casts, trolls, and still fishes for trout and bass in western lakes. When seeking members of the sunfish family, such as bluegills, he casts and still fishes from an outboard or drifting boat. He doesn't troll.

FLY AND SPINNING RODS

If the angler elects to use a spinning or fly rod for boat fishing he should not troll unless it is with a wet fly near the surface. His equipment is not made for it. With light casting equipment he should be primarily interested in reaching fish near the surface or to a depth of not more than 20 feet, fish swimming close to the shore, near ledges, in underwater vegetation areas, and around large rocks and logs. The best way to reach these areas from a boat is to cast toward the shoreline.

Fishing is seldom good in the deep waters of a lake unless the lures are allowed to go far down. In such cases a fly or spinning rod can be still-fished with a baited hook down to depths of 50 feet. But they should not be trolled because the shafts of the delicate rods are too limber and the reels are not built to hold up against the dragging weight of a line and weighted lure for long periods.

PLUG RODS

The lake fisherman's favorite boat rod is the short, sturdy plug-casting rod which has the kind of flexi-

bility needed for this type of fishing. Measuring about 5 to 6 feet the shaft is strong enough to handle the strain put upon rods for trolling. The reel is the rugged, level-wind type which also stands the abuse of trolling. The line measures about 15 pound test monofilament. This outfit is easy to use and enables a fisherman to act fast when he hooks a fish (or snag) because the rod, reel and fairly heavy line work well together in an emergency. They also work well for casting.

In addition to being ideal for trolling the plug casting rod is designed primarily to handle surface, subsurface, and deep-running plugs as well as spoons. These lures are often too heavy for the more flexible and longer-shafted spinning and fly rods to handle.

The term "rod action" describes the bend a rod-shaft takes with a given load. A favorite plug rod among boatmen has a flexible tip with a fairly stiff butt.

FAST TIP ACTION—
GOOD FOR CASTING
OR TROLLING.

LIMBER SHAFT
ACTION—PRIMARILY
FOR CASTING.

Before casting off, boat fishermen should have a plan for fishing, and should have the proper equipment to carry it out. The boat should be equipped for safety, too.

The weight and action of the trolling rod, size of the reel, and strength of the line and leader depend upon the kind of fishing being done.

Naturally, if a man uses a heavy sinker to carry his lure to a 50 foot depth the pull between his lure in the water and the moving boat will be far greater than if he were fishing a lure near the surface and no heavy sinkers were used.

It is not uncommon to find deep trolling in some lakes performed with the heavier salt water outfits which can support a large sinker and 100 feet of line being trolled at a 50 foot depth. This is much too heavy a job for light equipment to handle.

TROLLING IN A BOAT

Before casting off, a fisherman should have a plan in mind for his cruising. For example, he should have a fair idea of the lake's contour and where its primary ledges exist so he can follow them during his trolling. This may take hours of study to learn or he may be lucky in procuring a contour map of the lake which shows the ledge areas. (See the section, "Shore fishing for trout.")

Then he starts fishing slowly by throttling down his motor to minimum speed. As he proceeds he lets out line so the lure can sink to about 10 to 20 feet along the primary ledge. A sinker about four feet from his lure will probably be needed to help carry it down.

On clear, calm days a trolling lure is generally fished with a long line because the water's calmness requires a maximum of camouflage.

On windy, choppy days a shorter line with heavier sinker gets best results because the combination gives the lure better stability in choppy conditions.

Trolling is done at a slow speed. Occasionally, when there is no action a boatman may want to explore other depths than the one he has been fishing at a given speed. This can be done by changing the boat's direction. A sharp turn, for example, will ease the pull on the lure and allow it to sink deeper. By speeding up his motor he can bring the lure closer to the surface. These experiments can be conducted without taking the lure from the water—an important thing to do because it is a lure in water that catches fish and not out of it.

When netting a fish from a boat, the angler braces himself in a position of good balance, then carefully leads the fish head-first into a partially submerged net. A slightly lowered rod tip gives enough slack to permit an easy scooping motion.

As the fisherman trolls he may get a snag. Immediately he should stop his boat and then bring it over the place where the lure has been fouled. By measuring the length of line between boat and snag he gets a check on how deep he was trolling. It also enables him to look at landmarks along the lake's shore to locate the snag's position so he can be careful about it in the future.

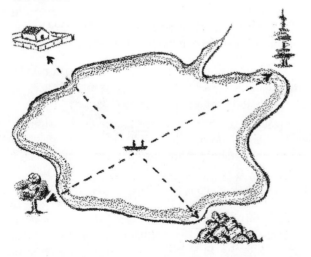

Fisherman should note landmarks so he later can find good fishing spots, or can avoid hidden snags.

NETTING A FISH FROM A BOAT

Many fishermen work long hours to hook and bring a fish to their boat, and then make a mistake which allows their prize to get away.

The best way to handle a rod when bringing a fish close to the boat is to hold the rod approximately horizontal to the water's surface. This rod position gives maximum control against a fish's unexpected behavior. If he dives under the boat, line can be released instantly to take care of the maneuver. If he rushes toward the boat, the rod tip can be raised to keep line taut, compensating for the charge. If the fish jumps or twists erratically, the fisherman is in good position to move his rod in any direction.

As the skillful netter holds his rod almost horizontally, he carefully submerges his net, including the rim, in a quiet way that does not add much to the fish's fright. Then he maneuvers the fish so it swims over the rim, head-first. Only when it is encircled does the angler gently raise the net around the body and out of the water, with a scooping motion.

An inexperienced netter has several faults. First, he may fail to keep his net submerged. Instead, he will make wild stabs at his quarry in attempts to catch him. This procedure can help shake the fish free because too much pressure is put on the mouth, and the hook is torn out.

Also, it is important never to strike the fish's tail with the rim or netting. This sets up an explosive reaction in the muscles from tail to head, and produces the kind of last-minute fight that often helps a trout or bass to get loose. This is related to the third common error, of trying to net the fish as it swims away. Any fish should always be netted head first.

INSPECT THE BOAT

One of the most important and most neglected factors of boat fishing is a careful examination of the boat to make sure there are no fire hazards or leaks, there is equipment for bailing, oars and oar locks work, anchoring and life saving devices are ship-shape, and that a guarantee exists for a safe return trip under any conditions.

Western lakes can suddenly become treacherous. Therefore, a boatman should have himself briefed about unusual weather conditions that could occur on the lake he has chosen to fish. He should have a familiarity with motor or engine operation in case of mechanical trouble.

FISHING PRIORITY

Another important point for boatmen to remember is that boats should stay away from waters being used by shore fishermen. And, it should be added, water skiers and fast cruisers should respect the rights of boat fishermen. Among sportsmen, the latter has an accepted priority of position.

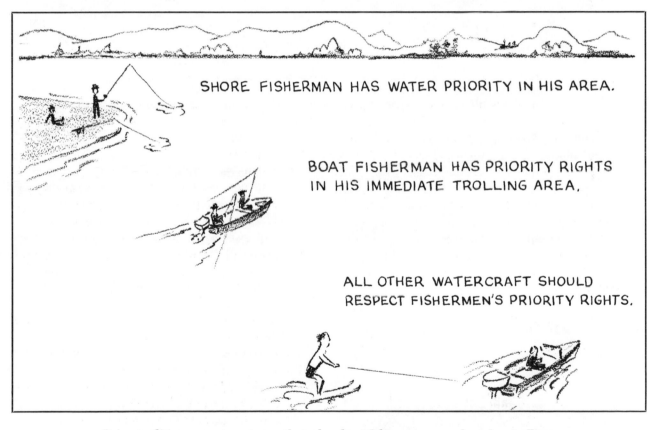

SHORE FISHERMAN HAS WATER PRIORITY IN HIS AREA.

BOAT FISHERMAN HAS PRIORITY RIGHTS IN HIS IMMEDIATE TROLLING AREA.

ALL OTHER WATERCRAFT SHOULD RESPECT FISHERMEN'S PRIORITY RIGHTS.

It is a tradition among sportsmen that when boat fishermen are anchored or trolling offshore, they have water priority. Fast boats and water skiers give them room.

Gamefish of the West

Many veteran anglers know the habits of their favorite gamefish better than the fish do. The following pages contain some useful information on the specific habits of the most popular Western gamefish.

Trout

The name trout shelters several fish, most of which are easily distinguishable from other members of the family. Either their appearances vary to a great degree, or their habits do. This section describes the varieties commonly caught in Western waters.

BROOK TROUT

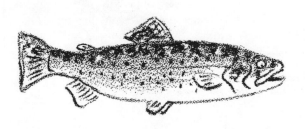

The original range of the brook trout was in the cold, clear waters of the Atlantic coast streams from Labrador south. Transplanted west, the brook has thrived in the high, cool waters of the great mountain ranges.

Brooks are careless feeders, and they cannot tolerate water temperatures of 75° or more. For these reasons they do not prosper in heavily fished lowland streams. However, brooks planted in remote, cold mountain lakes do quite well. In such places they can hide, keep cool, and find an abundance of insects without hooks inside. Also, the brook trout will spawn in the seepage areas or springs of high elevation lakes, while other trout require the running waters of a stream to propagate. The main trouble with planting them in lakes is that they multiply rapidly, outstripping food supplies, thus stunting their growth.

The back and upper sides of a brook trout are dark with wavy patterns of deep and olive green. There are also red spots on the sides, often with bluish rings around them. However, these may be indistinct in certain water conditions. A white and black stripe is on the fore-edge of the lower fins.

Behavior: The brook does not like rough going and has the habit of hiding behind obstacles in a current. In summer he lurks in deep pools and shady places because he suffers more in warm water than rainbows or browns.

Brooks are not regarded as smart feeders. When hungry they hit what attracts them, and the variety is wide. They feed on insects throughout their lives, starting with plankton when one inch long and working up through small insects into the fly category. This makes them excellent prospects for a fly fisherman's tackle, especially when the angler uses gaudy patterns of reds, whites, blues, and oranges instead of the realistic colors that seem to attract other species of trout.

BROWN TROUT

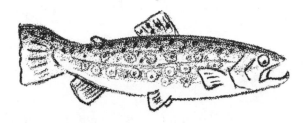

Browns are adaptable to a wide range of waters. They reproduce actively in the wild state, and since they have a good tolerance to heat (they can endure in water temperatures of 83°), cold, and water pollution, they seldom reach the fished-out stage. They are also known as Loch Levens and German Browns.

Browns are wary fish and frequently live a longer life than the more reckless rainbows or brooks. Consequently, fish ranging 8 to 12 pounds are not uncommon. In the Logan River of Utah a brownie weighing 37¾ pounds was landed in 1937. Under favorable stream conditions the brown's yearly growth rate is something like this: 3½, 6, 10, 14, 16, and 18 inches.

Color is usually dark olive to greenish brown on the back, shading to golden brown on the sides, and white or yellow on the belly. Rather large dark spots appear on the back and sides. Red spots surrounded by a light halo appear profusely over the upper part of the body. This is the only trout with both black and red spots on its body.

Behavior: The brown is a homebody. He likes to choose a spot behind the protective covering of a log or bank and stay in that immediate vicinity for the rest of his life.

When feeding he is inclined to move to the front or side of his covering where the current divides to pass around it, perhaps because he can get a better look at approaching food.

A favorite place to find him in daytime is beneath an undercut bank. Here he takes position in a pocket where a fast stream of water can pour over his back while the place in which he lies is almost still. From this position he waits for food and when he sees it he can make a fast move to grab it.

The trick for catching browns is to use a short line and present the leader so the lure can float fairly close to the pocket with no tell-tale drag of leader against water. When the brown strikes, the fisherman should pull his fish over the lip of the protective pool or pocket and get him out into the stream and away from snags. After being hooked he will try to return home, where he might have a chance to break the leader. Therefore, it is the job of the angler to keep a firm line so as to steer him away from the spot.

CUTTHROAT TROUT

The cutthroat ranges from northern California to Alaska, and cast into Wyoming and Colorado. In general, there are two types. One is the pure stream type, which likes cold streams and high, cool lakes. The other is the sea-run edition, which takes advantage of both freshwater and saltwater resources during his life.

The stream or lake cutthroat looks like other trout except for its bright red or orange "trademark" on the throat. This is the bloody looking slash mark that gives the fish its name.

When the sea-run cutthroat first enters fresh water from the salt, he is silvery and shiny. As maturity progresses and he swims upstream the fish takes on a brilliant coloration with pink and red gill covers, vivid black spots, and the red slash on his throat.

He is not a pugnacious fish and may fail to compete successfully for living space against the rainbow or brown. Also he tends to lose his identity through hybridizing with other trout.

Behavior: In mountain streams and lakes the cutthroat has similar behavior patterns to the rainbow and brown.

The sea-run type is different. He goes downstream to take up residence in a tidewater lagoon and grows rapidly, often attaining a length of 12 to 18 inches. Along the lagoon shoreline he takes a fly avidly. Large hooks can be used, up to No. 4, and the flies are generally streamers. During the day, spin fishermen get the most fish.

In July and on through late winter the sea-runs ascend streams to find their favorite small tributaries for spawning. Because they continue eating while enroute to their spawning grounds they are generally in prime condition when caught. When actually spawning they become emaciated, but soon recover.

Cutthroat are seldom caught in deep water. They prefer stream depths no greater than 10 feet, and are an excellent fish for a fly caster to go after along shorelines.

DOLLY VARDEN TROUT

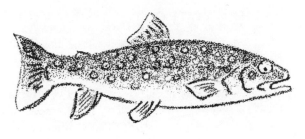

The Dolly Varden is native to the Pacific slope, and is classified as a near relative to the brook. (Both are chars, easily distinguished from other trout by the absence of teeth in the roofs of their mouths).

He is considered a glutton among trout, and eats almost anything, including the spawn of other fish. The reputation of destructive habits has not made the Dolly Varden a popular fish in spite of its pretty name.

The Dolly Varden is found mostly from Oregon into Alaska and east into Idaho and Montana. The fish has a strong migrating instinct and likes to leave his home stream for visits to the ocean or a large lake, depending upon where he is located. Where he has become landlocked in large lakes he has been mistaken frequently for the lake trout.

In small streams the Dolly Varden weighs ½ to 1 pound. In larger streams he ranges 2 to 4 pounds. In large lakes and nearby tributaries he may weigh from 8 to 15 pounds.

The overall color is a greenish brown with small orange and red spots dotting the back and sides. The spots are larger on the sides.

Behavior: In streams he prefers quieter or protected waters, much like the brook trout. In a pool he

will lie on the bottom and is a good prospect for bait. In lakes he likes the ridges near dropoffs into deep waters.

He puts up a fair battle against a hook, but is not so determined as other trouts.

GOLDEN TROUT

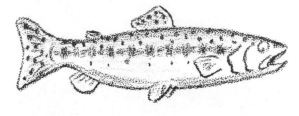

The typical golden trout in its natural home in the high Sierra Nevada Mountains is a brightly colored fish with distinctive shades of yellow and rose red on the lower sides and belly. The cheeks and pectoral, ventral, and anal fins are often red. The spotting is distinctive, being well defined against a clear background.

In some waters the golden and rainbow will hybridize and a wide variety of color variations will result.

The golden trout is considered a specimen trout because of its rarity and colorful beauty. It appeared originally in the high mountains of the Kern River drainage of California's Sierra Nevada Mountains. Its glamour and rarity have created wide interest and so during the past years it has been successfully transplanted to other Western mountain areas where cold, clear waters exist and the elevations average 8,500 to 11,000 feet. The golden prospers best in high areas with thin air. However, some are found occasionally as low as 6,300 feet.

Since the golden is a high altitude coldwater trout and spends much of its life in water temperature not favorable for active feeding and subsequent growth, the fish does not grow to large size. In small creeks and streams he will average only ½ to 1 pound. In lakes he will run larger. Because of their rarity few records are available about the largest goldens caught to date. It is surmised that 4 to 5 pounds is tops.

Behavior: In creeks and streams he demands a high degree of water clarity, gin-clear so to speak. He prefers pools to rapids and seems to combine the brook trout's liking for quiet water with the home-loving nature of the brown, which likes to settle in a protective pocket near a bank.

In lakes he prefers rocky shores where the water is sparkling clear and ledges drop into deep water.

His food is composed of insects, larvae, flies, the spawn of other fish, and from time to time worms.

Anglers who fish for golden trout seem to have the best luck with fly casting, using dry flies in early season and wet flies later. Spoons get late-season, sub-surface action, too. Most anglers willing to make the extreme effort to reach remote golden country are accomplished fly fishermen, and this may explain why flies are thought to be superior to other lures.

LAKE TROUT

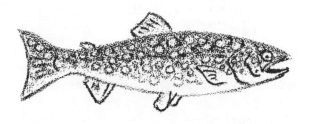

Lake trout are also known as the Mackinaw. They are large trout, ranging up to 50 or more pounds in their favorite mid-continent range. In the West, a big lake trout is in the 15 to 20-pound range.

They are dusky gray in color, darker above than below. Their sides are mottled with gray spots.

The lake trout enjoys colder water than other trouts.

Behavior: In summer, they prefer the cold depths of lakes, at 40 to 150 feet deep, where the water ranges from 40 to 50°. Summer fishermen troll for them with weighted lines and fairly heavy sinkers to get their lures down to where they think the fish are cruising. A good bait is a small fish imitation.

When hooked and pulled to the surface quickly, the change in water compression causes the lake trout's swim bladder to expand to such an extent that an unnatural buoyancy results. The fish cannot regain the depths if he fights free of the hook. Instead he will flap helplessly on the surface.

These are the first fish to visit a lake shoreline after a spring thaw. They feed voraciously on insects and crustaceans to break their winter fast, and give excellent action on light tackle for about two weeks. As soon as the water begins to warm, they return to the lake depths, where they remain until fall, their spawning time, when they come near shore to feed in preparation for the long winter.

This now-you-see-him-now-you-don't behavior is very frustrating to city fishermen who get word the trout are biting like crazy, and make a hurried trip to get to the "hot" lake just a day or so too late.

RAINBOW TROUT

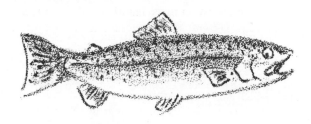

The rainbow is referred to as a Western native, which he is. However, because Western conditions are so varied and the rainbow has adapted himself to a wide range of them, his habits, coloring, and other characteristics are hard to pin down.

The size of an average stream rainbow is seldom record-breaking in any general sense. However, certain members of the family do get fairly large. The steelhead, which lives in the sea, and the kamloops, which does especially well in lakes, often reach weights of 20 pounds or slightly more.

The average rainbow is colored olive to greenish blue on top and silvery below. Black spots vary in size from pinpoint to $\frac{1}{8}$-inch in diameter, and are found on the upper half of the head, body, and tail. There are no red spots. The lateral band is usually conspicuous, and in red to violet. A "wild" or native rainbow is apt to be more highly colored than a recently planted hatchery fish. Also, their wide distribution has caused variations in marking.

Behavior: In most cases, the rainbow is a wanderer. Those found in high headwaters tend to share the stay-at-home qualities of the brook trout. Those that live farther downstream tend to be restless travelers. Almost all rainbows prefer open water. If planted in a small stream not to his liking, a rainbow often moves downstream to find more water.

He loves fast water, and is especially at home in small, sheltered pockets behind 12-inch or larger boulders where water flows so fast it gets foamy white. He loves to take station beside a current or riffle where food passes.

Rainbows weighing less than a pound feed primarily on insects, crustaceans, and plankton. They also eat small fish. Large rainbows are carnivorous, and feed heavily on small fish as well as the other types of food.

Since the rainbow is primarily an insect feeder, he will take wet or dry flies readily. Best results come from the smaller hooks, Nos. 10, 12, and 14.

Salmon

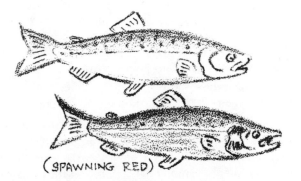

To this point, there has been no mention of salmon as a freshwater gamefish. He is not, in the pure sense, but his ventures into freshwater to spawn provide great sport for a brief period each year for light tackle fishermen.

Five species of salmon are native to the Pacific coast: King, silver, sockeye, pink, and chum. There are many other names for these fish noted below. Only the first two are of great concern to sport fishermen, and only they are described at length.

The king's smaller brother is called the silver salmon. Also known as the coho, its spawning runs occur in fall and winter. Silvers are smaller, in the 5 to 15 pounds range with about an 8-pound average.

KOKANEE

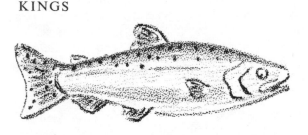

KINGS

(SPAWNING RED)

The big fellow of the salmon gamefish family is called the king or Chinook. The latter name comes from the Chinook tribe of Indians who lived luxuriously off the fish along the Columbia River.

Also known as the tyee salmon, spring salmon, and quinnat salmon, the king can be found ascending rivers in spring and fall.

Kings are big fish. They rarely weigh less than 10 pounds and sometimes near 100 pounds as they start leaving the ocean to spawn. The average is 15 to 25 pounds but every fisherman lives hopefully for the day he can tie into at least a 50-pounder and, of course, land him.

The young kings may go to sea during the first year or remain at least a year in the streams before swimming seaward. Growth is rapid in the sea and maturity averages in the fourth or fifth years at weights from 10 to 50 pounds. Males who mature in second and third years are called jacks. Small, immature fish of both sexes which start for the sea and then swim back upstream instead are referred to as grilse. They average 2 to 3 pounds while jacks range 2½ to 4 pounds.

A small relative of the king and silver is the freshwater kokanee salmon. This 12-incher is important in land-locked waters of Idaho, Montana, Oregon, and Washington because it multiplies well and is used both as a good forage fish for other fish to eat and a tasty gamefish for anglers to catch.

Kokanee have adapted themselves to inland waters because they thrive on plankton. They do well in reservoirs where the water levels change and food becomes scarce. This ability to thrive makes them excellent forage fish on which other gamefish can live.

Kokanee are related to the ocean-going sockeye, but are smaller.

HABITS

Pacific salmon return to the streams of their birth to spawn. The female digs her nest, known as a "redd" and deposits her eggs in the clean gravel of a river bottom while her male companion fertilizes them.

There the eggs adhere to sand and tiny rocks and are continually washed and supplied with oxygen by the pure waters of the stream.

After a period, which varies according to water temperature and other conditions, the eggs hatch into small fish which work their way up through the gravel to the open water.

There is no definite time for young salmon to flex their muscles and begin the long swim to sea. It varies with the species. King salmon start migrating to sea as small fry, soon after hatching. Silvers may wait as long as a year before they swim to sea. However, once they are in the ocean they both live on marine life until three, four, or five years of age. Then they return to the waters from which they started to complete their life cycle.

FEEDING

Perhaps one of the most important things a fisherman should know about salmon is that when the fish starts returning from the sea and tastes fresh water his throat automatically begins to close. So much so that within a short time it is an effort for him to swallow food. Later, he can't get anything down his throat.

To an angler, this is important, because after entering fresh water a salmon is not considered an active feeder. On the contrary, it disregards food and relies entirely upon a reservoir of body fat to supply the needed energy and strength to reach the spawning grounds.

When a salmon is caught upstream and his stomach is cut open for examination it will be empty.

Fishermen often ask, if a salmon doesn't feed in fresh water why does it strike a lure or bait?

The answer must be theoretical because to date no one has been able to talk to a king or silver and learn things first-hand. Apparently they have a lingering desire to eat even after it is impossible for them to swallow.

However, it is logically assumed that because a salmon has so strong an urge to reach its spawning grounds it will fight anything that gets in the way. This includes other fish, rocks, floating debris, flashing spinners, spoons, plugs, flies, or gobs of bait which may bump its tail or nose, or threaten interference with the journey's progress.

The point for a fisherman to remember is that a salmon is inclined to fight or strike at objectionable objects because of anger or fright. This is one of the reasons so many salmon nearing their spawning grounds are marked with white scars. They are the scars of struggle. The secret of salmon fishing in a stream, therefore, is to throw something in their way that bothers them.

There is one feeding exception where fresh water fishermen can cast for salmon and get results.

This is in tidewater lagoons. In these brackish waters the continued presence of salt water can sometimes delay the throat-closing action of salmon. This is especially true with silvers.

In such a place, the fish may still be hungry and eat bait or hit lures, including flies.

SPAWNING

Many fishermen mistakenly believe that a salmon dies after spawning because it uses all its energy resources to reach a far-away spawning area and when the eggs are finally delivered the fish expires from complete exhaustion.

Although motherhood is admittedly heroic and publicity photographs showing salmon leaping over barriers are full of drama, the fact is that exercise related to egg-laying by salmon is not the underlying cause for death. For example, many well-conditioned salmon lay eggs in native streams within a few miles of the sea, after an easy swim. They also die.

The reason salmon die after spawning is because getting ready to spawn creates a physiological degenerative process in their organs. This degeneration reaches a climax as the eggs are laid and fertilized. Death sets in immediately afterward.

Steelhead

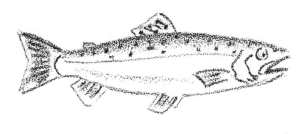

The steelhead—a sea-going rainbow trout—is, like the salmon, a special case. His range is small and the season is short, but he is an experience the trout fisherman should not do without in his fishing lifetime.

The following section is devoted to a brief description of his habits, and the habits of the hardy fishermen who try to catch him every winter in the coldwater rivers of Washington, Oregon, and northern California.

Steelhead range in size from 5 to 20 pounds. They usually enter the ocean when one or two years old, and spend from one to three years at sea before returning to fresh water.

When it is time to spawn, a steelhead almost always returns to the stream in which he was naturally hatched, or to the waters in which he was liberated if he was hatchery-raised.

A casual glance will not always tell the difference between a salmon and a steelhead that is new to fresh water. They can be separated by the way they fight a hook. The salmon fights much of his battle beneath the water's surface. The steelhead keeps the fighting characteristics of a trout, which he is. His athletic gyrations create an above-the-water circus anglers refer to as "walking on his tail."

Once the fish is caught, there are two other quick tests. Grasp the fish around the base of his tail. If it slips through the hand, he is a steelhead; if it is easily held, the fish is a salmon. The tail of a salmon is forked and fairly rigid. The steelhead's tail is close to square and quite soft. Also, the inside of a steelhead's mouth is white while a salmon's is gray or blackish.

STEELHEAD SPAWNING HABITS

Unlike the salmon, a steelhead continues eating after leaving the ocean. His appetite may be finicky because he is naturally nervous in his new stream environment, and nervousness will reduce any animal's appetite, including a human's. However, the fact remains that steelhead do continue eating after entering freshwater from the ocean.

After reaching the spawning grounds to drop and fertilize eggs, these huge 20 to 36 inch trout may return to the sea to start another cycle. This is because the spawning process does not create the fatal physiological decay of organs it does in salmon.

Therefore, if a steelhead feels physically capable of another long sojourn in the ocean he will make the trip.

If he doesn't he may spend the rest of his life at home, undoubtedly using some bitter fish language to complain about water pollution and other havoc caused by automobilists who fish or scatter debris from four-lane highways, which seem to parallel many steelhead streams.

Steelhead ascend Pacific Coast streams with salmon and will take flies or other lures. In most cases these baits must be presented so they bounce or float along the bottom of the area being fished.

The larger rivers, which have a constant flow of cold, snow-fed water throughout the year, have a summer run of small steelhead ranging from 3 to 5 pounds. Some tributary streams fed by cold springs support quantities of summer steelhead while the main river into which the tributary flows has no summer steelhead above the fork because the water in it is not cold enough for a steelie's liking.

In fall, when waters get colder, migrating fish are active in all coastal streams and their weights are as much as 20 pounds.

Smaller streams, such as the short ones located in the coastal mountains, generally have a low water level in summer and this gives the ocean tides a chance to build dams of sand across their mouths. Such a dam creates a lagoon of brackish water which is fed by the stream's trickle.

These dammed creeks and rivers need heavy rains to produce enough high water to break through the ocean's sand barriers. In late fall and winter, when this occurs, waiting steelhead enter the lagoon and begin swimming upstream. This starts the season of winter steelhead fishing. Fish in the 10 to 15 pound range are not uncommon, 20 pounds is still about top weight.

FALL FISHING

The fall season begins along the Washington coast in July and progresses south from August through November in larger coastal streams and their tributaries.

At this time of year the art of fishing for steelies follows the same general technique as that used for regular trout fishing because fall-run steelhead hold the same patterns of behavior as trout, which they are.

An angler who knows how to fish his riffles, holes, and currents for rainbows, brooks, or browns will have good luck by using the same tactics for fall-run steelhead.

The major difference between ordinary trout fishing and steelhead fishing is the fisherman's choice of hook and leader sizes. For a 10 to 12-inch trout, a favorite hook size is the small No. 12 with a leader of 2 or 3 pound test. For steelhead, flyfishing is done with a larger hook size such as No. 6, and stronger leader, 6 pound test. For bait fishing, use a small No. 10 hook with a single egg.

For spin fishing, at least an 8-pound test line should be used with spinners and plugs. For fishing with a plug outfit No. 4 or 6 hooks and 8 to 10-pound test leaders are suggested.

In fall, the riffles and bubbling water of the larger steelhead streams are often good for flies. The pools and eddies are best for bait and lures. Swift water is for bait. It takes a fair-sized sinker to carry the bait down in fast current and artificial lures without extra weight don't produce consistently.

In fall extra-long casts, 60 feet or more, are often necessary. Steelhead country tackle shops stock special gear for this kind of fishing.

WINTER STEELHEAD

The winter season for steelhead runs from November through February in most regions.

At this time of year the water is colder, frequently murky, and occasionally turbulent. Fish ascend these streams with caution because the waters do not promote the kind of peace and quiet a frightened, migrating fish would like to find.

At this time of year steelhead fishing seems most successful in pools, holes, and eddies. Those are the places steelies can rest and recuperate before they again start battling the swift currents leading to spawning grounds.

During such rest periods they are inclined to feed. In winter, the favorite bait is a large gob of roe, held together with cheesecloth, a piece of nylon stocking, or a wrapping of thread. Attached to a No. 4 or 6 hook, the bait is called a "strawberry" because it looks like one.

There are hundreds of secrets and theories about fishing for winter steelhead. Perhaps the most important thing a fisherman should recognize is not related to fishing at all—this is to keep warm.

A winter fisherman along the Pacific Coast should wear extra-warm garments, have rubber boots or waders he knows will not leak, carry gloves and other accessories to provide protection against icy winds and other exposure.

Not infrequently the weather turns so cold on a steelhead stream that the drops of water resting in rod guides and reel will freeze. Fingers, feet, the nose, and chest are especially vulnerable to the cold. This is the kind of climate that can become awfully uncomfortable and a man who feels that way will stop fishing. He will return home without fish and be forced to use his excuse box overtime so he can explain why he didn't catch anything.

Other fishes

"Other fishes" may seem like a high-handed way to treat such fine gamefish as the black basses, striped bass, shad, and walleyes. But bass already have been thoroughly examined in earlier chapters. The other fish noted here are not widely distributed enough, or highly regarded enough to require lengthy treatment.

BLACK BASS

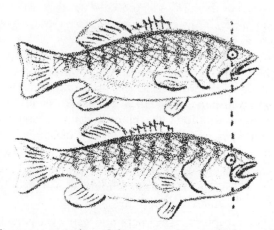

These are nesting fishes, members of the sunfish family. As waters start warming in spring, they build nests from mud and sticks on the bottom. The small fish hatched in the nest eat plankton. Away from the nest, young fish begin to favor tiny water animals and insects. As adults, black bass add small fish (including their own young) to the menu.

Largemouth: These rugged fish like warmth. The average largemouth feeds best between 70 and 80°. Depending upon water conditions and available food he grows between spring and autumn from two inches to seven inches in length. The second year he will reach eight to twelve inches.

Largemouth reach as much as 22 pounds in the warm waters of Arizona and southern California. However, 3 to 4 pounds is considered good-sized in the West as a whole.

These fish prefer quiet water with soft bottom and plenty of vegetation for cover and as a storehouse for food.

Smallmouth: It is hard to tell the difference between largemouths and smallmouths because their shape and coloring are similar. The smallmouth actually has a smaller mouth, but it is not very much smaller.

It is easier to tell the difference between the two by looking at the places from which they are caught. The smallmouth likes 70° water, gravel or boulder-strewn bottom, and fair current. He has many of the living habits of a brook trout. He is slimmer and smaller than a largemouth of the same age. On the average he weighs 2 to 3 pounds.

BLUEGILL

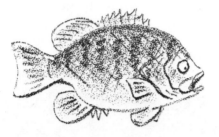

These oval-shaped fish like lakes and ponds with moderate vegetation. The bluegill is not a large fish, running ½-pound or less. His meat is delicious.

Bluegills travel in schools and they love to swim in places that supply them with protective cover. When a fisherman finds a school he will find fast action for a number of minutes.

They are prolific spawners and can over-populate an area of water if they are not harvested occasionally. When planted with largemouth bass the latter eats them as forage fish and this helps keep down the number of bluegills.

CATFISH

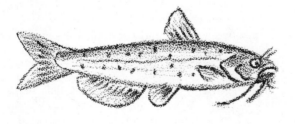

Catfish can be easily recognized by scaleless bodies, long barbels at the mouth, and sharp, heavy pectoral fins and dorsal spines.

They feed on both plant and animal food. To some, they are scavengers feeding on dead fish, frogs, clams, etc.

As with most warmwater fishes, at hatching time the male assumes care of the nest and eggs. A conscientious parent, he sticks around for several weeks after hatching to make certain the youngsters don't get involved in trouble.

White catfish like things quiet. They seek large, slow rivers in both fresh and brackish waters. They do not grow much above 8 pounds.

Channel catfish prefer larger rivers and lowland lakes with fairly clean bottoms of sandy gravel and boulders. However, they are adaptable and have thrived when planted in muddy areas such as parts of the Colorado River.

The channel "cat" is popular for several reasons. His size ranges from 5 to 30 pounds. His meat is so delicious he makes a tasty dish for any angler or gourmet who likes to eat fish. He is clean and gives a good account of himself when fighting a hook.

Baits for catfish are anything in the animal or vegetable line, especially with a strong, sour smell. Catfish fishermen generally refer to their favorite baits as "concoctions." Angleworms and night crawlers are favorite natural baits and so are live minnows in areas where they are legal.

CRAPPIE

There are two crappies. These are the white and the black. They are frequently mistaken for black bass. Crappie thrive best in the warm, quiet waters of sloughs, lakes and slow rivers. Black crappie prefer clear water whereas white crappie like turbid water and mud bottom. They range to 12 inches long, weighing ½ to 1 pound.

They are prolific fish and tend to overpopulate waters. When this happens they give the black bass so much competition for food that the latter begin to suffer.

Crappie are considered good gamefish for the table, whatever their faults may be.

SHAD

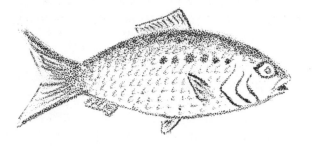

The shad spends his life at sea but migrates annually up coastal rivers to spawn. He may grow as long as 30 inches and reach a weight up to 12 pounds. Color is metallic blue on the back and silvery on the sides with a half dozen black spots in a row beginning at the gill. He has a deep body, and a tender mouth a hook can tear through easily.

The shad is famous for its roe among gourmet diners. Along with caviar from the sturgeon, shad roe is a bait that catches more human beings than many human beings care to admit. They can frequently be detected by the size of their waistlines, however.

Behavior: During shad runs to spawning grounds fishermen frequently have best luck with small, bright colored flies. Spinners also hook the shad. Both lures are fished below the surface.

Since his mouth is so tender and he fights a real battle a shad takes considerable skill to land. Any fisherman who can hook and land a good catch with fly casting equipment is entitled to call himself an expert angler.

STRIPED BASS

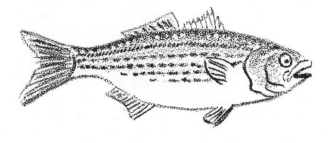

Although the striped bass is regarded primarily as a saltwater species he is anadromous and lives equally well in either salt or fresh water. An import from the Chesapeake area to the San Francisco Bay region, the striper has thrived in the West and is now moving up and down the Pacific coast.

As a result of studies made of how and why striped bass thrived so well in the fresh water delta area of upper San Francisco Bay, it was decided to experimentally plant them in some inland fresh water lakes.

These landlocked fish have done well and offer excellent sport. If and when the striper's spawning problems in lakes are eliminated, the term "landlocked striper" may be adopted to go along with the term "landlocked salmon" to indicate that a former saltwater fish has taken up a new abode far away from the sea.

The spawning problem for the striped bass is that striper eggs are semi-buoyant and need currents to keep them in suspension to insure a successful hatch. Otherwise they sink into the mud and their life is stifled.

STURGEON

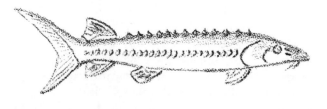

The sturgeon is by far the largest member of the Western family of fresh-water fishes. The record book shows one taken from the Columbia River weighing more than 1,800 pounds.

There are several species of sturgeon; but in Western fresh waters ranging from Alaska to San Francisco Bay it is the white sturgeon that anglers hook into.

Catching a sturgeon always comes as something of a surprise. Because of their camouflage and habit of lying close to the bottom, they are never seen. However, an angler who bottom fishes as he does for catfish or striped bass occasionally feels as if he has snagged into a sunken log. As he reels in he may feel movement, and then as the sturgeon decides to break away, things pop. A hundred or more pounds of battling meat on the end of a fishing line is a challenge.

Sturgeon prefer to lie on clean bottom. When spawning, the female seeks deep holes with currents. Some of them live to be 150 years old, so they must be rather smart or extra careful.

Western Fishing: State-by-State

The population of the West has predictably taxed the capacities of its resources, including freshwater fish.

Despite the West's sensational growth, the angling sport must still be rated from good to excellent. Admittedly it is not always good in streams along a busy four-lane highway, or near a popular resort. But it is still quite satisfactory within a mile's walk from a concrete artery or a vacationer's hotel. Modern fish management in the Western states has maintained large fish populations in many streams and lakes.

Complaints about waters being fished-out frequently come from fishermen who are disappointed because they find no magic in the equipment they bought from a persuasive fishing tackle salesman, or come from men who have acquired the habit of riding to the edge of the water they plan to fish. Fishing always will require practiced skills. And a good freshwater fisherman accepts the fact that his sport involves a certain amount of exercise to reach a good spot.

He does not forget that in the "good old days" nearly everybody walked, rode a horse, or took a long train ride to reach a favorite stretch of water. Without this sort of effort they didn't have good fishing luck in those days, either.

The following is a summary compilation of basic fishing information in the West. It isn't meant as a guide to specific fishing waters, but it will help in the search.

This book lacks the endless amount of room needed to list specific travel destinations for fishermen. Good fishing waters are everywhere. One of the best source books for fishermen out on a fishing expedition in unfamiliar territory is **Sunset's** *Western Campsite Directory.*

Arizona

For a long, long time Arizona was known as an area where the sun was hot and the country extremely dry. As fishermen saw it, Arizona was at the end of the line when Mother Nature passed out gamefish water.

But the picture has changed. Now there is water, an abundance of it compared with only a few years ago. Large dams have been built across rivers and water runoff areas. A system for the release of this water for power and irrigation has formed new fishable streams. These new, man-made waters have been stocked heavily with gamefish. Small projects on farms and in cities have been built also to further increase the collection and control of water.

As a result of these conservation programs much of the Arizona countryside has changed from dry, hot desert into green square miles of rich farm lands. Industrious Arizonans have made up for any oversight of Mother Nature in the matter of fine fishing waters.

TYPES OF FISH IN ARIZONA

Because of Arizona's climate and reservoir system the most popular type of fishing is for warmwater species. The most sought-after is the largemouth black bass.

In these rich, warm areas where a bass can eat 12 months a year, the bronzeback will reach 6 pounds while his northern brothers in colder lakes struggle to reach a weight of 1 pound.

Arizona's warmwater fishing falls into two major areas: one is the lakes of the Salt River region from Phoenix east; the second is the Colorado River complex starting at the lower end of the Grand Canyon and proceeding south.

Smallmouth bass do well in the Verda River watershed and lower reaches of the Colorado.

Sunfish such as bluegills and crappie reach unusual sizes for their species and abound in Arizona waters. Channel catfish also prosper.

Trout fishing is found in a few streams rising in the central part of the state and extending east into the New Mexico boundary, and at the bases of huge dams where cold waters spill out to form stream temperatures to the trout's liking. For example, the cold waters pouring out of the depths of Lake Mead now provide excellent trout fishing below Hoover Dam.

ARIZONA SEASONS, LICENSES, AND LIMITS

Seasons: Fishing is uncomplicated in Arizona because there is no closed season on any fish species. The sport may be enjoyed at any time of the year and at any time of the day or night.

The best fishing seasons range from February into May and from September into December. During the warm June-August spell the hot sun drives fish into deep water and cool cover, and at such times they are harder to find and catch.

Licenses: License fees are $3 for residents' all-season; $9 for non-residents' all-season; $3 for the non-residents' 5-day license. Trout stamps are $2 for the non-resident, and there is a special Colorado River license, good for all Colorado river fishing, $10 for non-residents.

Agreements between the states of Arizona, California, and Nevada govern the fishing waters of the Colorado River complex. These detailed regulations are best understood once the fisherman is in the region.

Limits: The daily limit for catches of trout, kokanee salmon, black bass, and channel catfish is 10 fish. For striped bass in the Colorado River, the limit is 3.

Further information may be obtained from the Department of Game and Fish, Phoenix.

British Columbia

Canada is big; only the Soviet Union and Red China are larger. Lying along the west coast of this enormous country is the Province of British Columbia, which occupies more space than the combined areas of Washington, Oregon, and California, and which stretches north from the U.S. border far past the southern tip of Alaska, and as far east as Montana.

Its vast, forest-blanketed expanse is criss-crossed by uncounted miles of streams and dotted by hundreds of lakes that both fish and fishermen enjoy.

Much of it is unspoiled country seldom or never visited by sportsmen. Many spots are inaccessible to automobiles, but can be reached by canoe, pack trip, or fly-in, after proper arrangements are made with Fish and Game offices or licensed guides.

For vacationing motorists who like their fishing waters to be handy, there are over 5,000 miles of paved highways and 10,000 miles of improved gravel roads reaching into park-like wilderness filled with prime gamefish lakes and streams. There are gasoline stations and housing accommodations along the way.

For campers, the Department of Recreation and Conservation has set aside areas throughout the Province as unspoiled parklands. In magnificent settings campers will find tables, tent space, garbage cans, fireplace, toilet facilities, and firewood available for their use.

TRAVELING TO BRITISH COLUMBIA

The trip to British Columbia is as easy as crossing the street after the traffic officer nods his approval. There are few lengthy examinations by border police, no requests for passports or proofs of innoculations. However, an American visitor should carry some type of proper identification such as credit cards, driving license, or other papers to facilitate re-entry into the United States.

And here is an important tip for motorists. In case of an accident British Columbia authorities impound the motorist's car unless he can furnish undisputed proof of adequate insurance coverage.

In accidents resulting in aggregate property damage of $250, or death or injury, the motorist needs a minimum coverage of $35,000 liability insurance. To be prepared for such a contingency many travelers obtain a B.C. Motor-Vehicle Liability Insurance Card (non-resident) from their insurance agent before they leave home. This insures them against the inconvenience of waiting while police authorities wire, write, or telephone their insurance company to confirm the fact they own adequate coverage. It also gives the holder added identification.

TYPES OF FISH IN BRITISH COLUMBIA

British Columbia is especially famous for salmon and trout. Its pure waters, in rich watersheds, encourage the growth of these species.

Salmon fishing for king and silver is confined to coastal streams. Anglers will find some degree of success the year around. However, the best king action begins in April and reaches its height in early fall.

Silvers start concentrating for their runs upstream in July and provide their best action in mid-fall.

One of the most famous places for salmon fishing is the Campbell River on the east coast of Vancouver Island. This is the location of the renowned Tyee Club, an organization of sportsmen which was founded to prescribe maximum and minimum tackle standards to achieve the ultimate in sport fishing with lightweight gear. Because of the Tyee Club's fame the king (or Chinook) salmon is also called the tyee. The club's program for tackle standards is now used or adapted for sport fishing all over the world.

Inland waters abound with the kokanee, a land-locked salmon, known as the sockeye in ocean waters. These fish average a pound and provide excellent sport as well as being a forage fish upon which larger gamefish feed.

The rainbow, cutthroat, and brown trouts are the three main species in British Columbia. The rainbow in the sea-run variety is the steelhead. The resident variety is generally the kamloops, the most important freshwater gamefish in the province.

The cutthroat in coastal areas may be either the sea-going or resident species and is called the coastal cutthroat. In southeastern B.C. it becomes the Yellowstone or mountain cutthroat.

Brown trout were introduced in 1932 and have thrived. They have become a prime favorite among fly fishermen because they are so wary they refuse to hit any bait except a lightweight lure. Anglers therefore display a catch of browns with much pride.

In addition to the aforementioned, there are also brook trout and others. Black bass have been introduced into some sections.

Detailed information on what to fish for and where can be obtained from the Department of Fish and Game, Victoria, B.C., or the Tourist Information Centers located in key cities.

SEASONS, LICENSES, AND LIMITS

Customs regulations allow a non-resident to enter the province with his fishing gear and other equipment, duty free. Fishing licenses can generally be obtained from the Canadian Customs Officer at the port of entry. They can also be obtained at other appropriate headquarters.

Licenses: License fees are $7 for non-resident anglers license for adults, $1 under 16 years; $3.50 for non-resident anglers license, Canadians only.

Limits: Daily limits in non-tidal waters are 12 trout or 2 over 20 inches long. In tidal waters the daily limits are 4 salmon or 8 grilse of under 3 pounds. Possession limit in most areas is total of 3-day catch.

For further information the British Columbia Sport-Fishing Regulations should be studied.

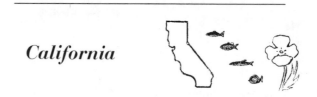

California

California is a state of superlatives. It has the longest coastline, more than 1,000 miles; some of the highest mountains, up to 14,495 feet; the lowest valleys, down to 282 feet below sea level; the most fishermen, 1½ million license holders; the highest waterfalls; the most people; the most species of freshwater fish, and many other firsts or mosts.

On the long axis of the state the 450-mile long Central Valley provides a drainage basin for the rivers which race from the Sierra Nevada mountains. To the Pacific come the fast coastal rivers from the western slopes of the coast ranges. Natural high

Sierra lakes, the multitude of new reservoir lakes ringing the Central Valley, and the warm water lakes of Southern California complete the picture. Taken together this variety of rivers and lakes provides as many kinds of water and as many kinds of fish as can be found everywhere else in the west.

The gigantic water programs of California's dams, canals, power projects, and community reservoirs have changed fishing conditions and will continue to bring new changes. Where once the state was famous among anglers as a land composed primarily of mountain streams, tumbling rivers and high, glacial lakes it is now becoming known for its huge artificial lakes. These are attractive waters where a man can wet a line and get some good fishing action while the family watches or plays in the area.

While the native Californian hasn't entirely embraced this type of fishing, millions of transplanted easterners and mid-westerners who grew up in lake areas are delighted with it. They understand it and enthusiastically support the growing program. And because there are fish in the lakes and fun in the areas, lake popularity is bound to grow.

TYPES OF FISH IN CALIFORNIA

California boasts about the variety of gamefish in its waters because every type of water environment is found in the state and fish management says appropriate fish plants have been made to take advantage of these conditions. In addition to a full range of trout varieties large and smallmouth bass, perch, catfish, and crappie are abundant.

Anadronous fish include salmon, steelhead, shad, striped bass, and cutthroat. The landlocked Salton Sea features the racy, saltwater corvina.

SEASONS, LICENSES, AND LIMITS

Seasons: Trout season varies because the state is so large. Generally speaking, it runs from early May through October. However, in some parts of the south where trout fishing conditions are poor there is no closed season. Warmwater fishing is all year.

Licenses: $3 fee for all-season residents' license; $3 non-resident for 10 days fishing; Boys and girls 15 years and younger require no license; 1 stamp is required for inland fishing, except for trout, at $1; 2 stamps are required for inland fishing, including trout, at $2.

Limits: 10 trout or salmon in combination but not more than 10 lbs. and one fish. Special rules apply to steelhead and salmon.

Fish other than trout and salmon range from a limit of 3 to no limit depending upon the species.

California publishes the country's most extensive copies of fishing literature. You may order single copies of hunting and sportfishing regulations free of charge, as well as maps, wildlife leaflets, and angler's guides. There is a charge for bulk orders and for certain other booklets. Write to: Office of Procurement, Documents Section, P. O. Box 20191, Sacramento, California 95820. Ask for the pamphlet "Vacation Aids" and the publication price list.

A 32-page booklet of California sport fishing regulations is available at all sporting goods stores or it and other excellent information may be obtained by writing Department of Fish and Game, 722 Capitol Avenue, Sacramento, California or visiting one of the department's many branch offices.

Colorado

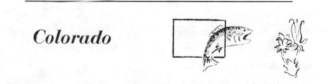

Colorado, the highest state in the Union, straddles the Rocky Mountains, where 1,500 peaks rise above 10,000 feet. The average altitude is 6,800 feet above sea level. Denver, the state's capital, is famous as "The Mile High City."

The Continental Divide, which forms a crest through the center of Colorado, divides the watersheds of the Pacific Ocean and the Gulf of Mexico.

In these mountains rise famous rivers such as the Colorado which flows southwest into the Gulf of California; the Snake which empties into the Columbia and finally the Pacific. The Platte and Republican rivers flow into the Mississippi; and the Rio Grande reaches the Gulf of Mexico. Nineteen states are supplied with water originating in Colorado, known as "The Mother of Rivers."

Along with other Western states, Colorado is actively conscious of growing fishing pressures caused by ever-increasing human population, more leisure time, accessibility to waters, shrinking fish habitat from road building, land use, pollution, four-wheel drive vehicles, better fishing tackle, and more fishermen. Therefore, it has adopted a program for improving lake fishing which now has the active attention of fish and game management. These lakes for public fishing are predominantly cold water; 1,502 are natural and 1,015 are man-made. Warm water reservoirs for public fishing total 154.

TYPES OF FISH IN COLORADO

For the fisherman this is great trout country. An estimated 11,300 miles of clear, cold water streams range in width from 1 foot to an awesome 300 feet. Public miles of fishing streams are 6,800 miles of 20 feet width or less, 2,550 miles of 21 feet to 100 feet width, and 250 miles of 101 feet to 300 feet width.

The rugged, mountainous sections of Colorado are the favorites of anglers. Here in picturesque settings are thousands of small streams in the 20 to 50-foot width range and many, many high altitude lakes in glacial cirques above or near the timberline. The rivers supply rainbow, brown, brook, grayling, and Colorado whitefish. The lakes specialize in rainbow, mackinaw, brook, and kokanee salmon.

Waters flowing into the eastern plains trace their ways through arid lands. Generally speaking, the best fishing in this area is in the man-made reservoirs. Bass, crappie, bluegill, and walleyed pike are the favorite species.

A fishing innovation in Colorado is the establishment of several fly-fishing-only and artificial-lure-only areas. These "quality" or "fish-for-fun" areas require that all trout under 12 inches must be released alive.

It is worth noting that several other western states are now adopting this sportsmanlike plan for certain streams.

COLORADO SEASONS, LIMITS

Seasons: Recently, the State of Colorado adopted a year-around season for all species of fish except for spawning area closures. This was done to spread the fishing pressure and reduce the average opening day "bring your own rock to stand on" fiasco.

However, it should be pointed out that Colorado has icy winters which automatically make thousands of miles of trout streams inaccessible, and the activity of fishes slows considerably.

Licenses: License fees are $4 for residents' all-season; $10 for the non-residents' all-season; $3.50 for the non-residents' 5-day permit (renewable).

Limits: In Colorado there are no size or weight limits on trout. Creel limits for trout are 6 from November 1 through May 31; 10 from June 1 through October 31. Warm water limits are bass, 10; walleye, and northern pike, 6; and, others, 30 in aggregate. There are no size limits on warm water species.

Idaho

Idaho is a country of high, snow-capped peaks, steep slopes covered with forests, deep valleys and canyons, more than 2,000 lakes, and a network of 35,000 miles of fishable streams.

In southern Idaho, Hell's Canyon, carved by the Snake River, is deeper than the Grand Canyon of the Colorado. The Shoshone Falls of this region are higher than Niagara Falls. In the north is the country of giant-sized lakes.

The forests, mountains, rivers, and lakes make the state a fine vacationland.

Important to fishermen is an examination of the record fish caught in Idaho. Each year rainbow, Dolly Varden, and mackinaw ranging in the 30-pound class receive public acclaim. Also, since most of the state is public domain, nearly all waters are available for public fishing although many are remote from any road. In the case of posted or fenced lands used for private agriculture or stock purposes, permission to use waters flowing through these regions should be obtained. Most large lakes and reservoirs have facilities for boats and other accommodations.

TYPES OF FISH IN IDAHO

Famous places in the northern Panhandle of large lakes are Lake Pend Orielle for huge kamloops rainbow; Priest Lake for mackinaw lake trout. The Salmon River and Silver Creek in the south central part are noted for fly fishing; the north fork of the Snake River and its tributaries in southeastern Idaho are outstanding producers of rainbows on bait or fly.

Other species of fish available to the angler are salmon, trout including steelhead, rainbow, cutthroat, brown, brook, and Dolly Varden. Warmwater species are also available in certain portions of the state and include: largemouth and smallmouth bass, perch, crappie, and channel catfish.

IDAHO SEASONS, LICENSES, LIMITS

Seasons: The Idaho fishing season is a late starter. Generally the fishing season opening is on the closest Saturday to June 1.

Many streams are high and roily in the early part of the season and bait is recommended under these conditions. The numerous lakes and small streams are the best producers.

As the waters begin clearing in mid-June fishing improves rapidly throughout the state and dry and wet flies along with other artificial lures get the fish. From mid-summer until the season's close on October 31, Idaho fishing is at its best.

Licenses: Residents' are $4 all season. Non-resident, seasonal is $15. Non-resident, 7-day fishing is $5. Non-resident, first day fishing is $2 and for each additional one-day of fishing it is $1 per day. A non-resident child of 14 years or under may fish without a license provided he is accompanied by a holder of valid license and fish taken by a child will be included in adult's bag limit. For further information, write the Department of Fish and Game, Boise.

Montana

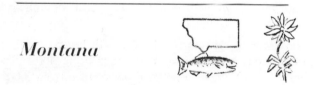

One of Montana's greatest treasures is its wealth of wildlife. From the prairies and badlands in the east to the rugged areas of western Montana where crystal-clear waters pour out of the Rocky Mountains, the state provides fishing in abundance, not only in numbers but also in a variety of fish.

Montana is traversed by four major streams—the Yellowstone, Missouri, Kootenai, and Clark's Fork of the Columbia. These streams, with their many tributaries and hundreds of connected lakes, offer to the angling enthusiast a diversity of fishing found in few other places of the United States.

The "blue-ribbon" streams, which are rated among the finest producers of scrappy gamefish in the United States, are: Big Hole River near Melrose; Rock Creek near Missoula; Madison River from Cliff Lake to Three Forks; Gallatin River from Eldridge to near Bozeman; Yellowstone River from Yellowstone National Park to Big Timber; Missouri River from Wolf Creek to Ulm, Missouri River from Lombard to Townsend.

In addition to the above mentioned waters there are another estimated 8,500 miles of beautiful trout streams tracing their ways through the state.

Lake fishermen get their action from two types: The man-made impoundments of eastern Montana's prairie lands and the natural lakes of the western portion which are too numerous to mention here.

TYPES OF FISH IN MONTANA

Montana is well-known for its excellent brown, rainbow, cutthroat, and brook trout fishing. Perhaps its prize specimen is the rare grayling which is found in the high, cold lakes of the west. Kokanee salmon, a one pounder which never leaves fresh water, also gives excellent sport.

Angling in Montana is popular among its natives in spring. In summer it is good to excellent, especially in the western portions of the state. Temperatures rarely reach 100 degrees in the mountainous areas and visiting anglers have wonderful sport. The best angling is in fall. At this time the famous brown (Loch Leven) trout make their annual spawning runs and during such movement provide great excitement. During this period they hit flies, lures, and bait and average from 3 to 8 pounds. Many larger ones are also taken. For the more virile anglers, winter fishing is popular. Through the ice, anglers fish the reservoirs and report good catches of perch, trout, and whitefish.

MONTANA LICENSES, LIMITS

Licenses: License fees are $3 for a residents' seasonal license; $10 for a non-residents' seasonal license; and $3 for the non-residents' 6-day license.

Limits: For trout, char, and grayling the daily limit is 10 fish, not to exceed 10 pounds and 1 fish. Twenty whitefish are allowed daily. Fifteen fish not exceeding 15 pounds and 1 fish are allowed daily for walleye pike, sauger, northern pike, and bass. For kokanee salmon, the daily limit is the same as trout except from October 1 to December 31 when 35 kokanees are allowed daily.

Further information about Montana fishing may be obtained from the Department of Fish and Game, Helena.

Nevada

Nevada's topography is composed of a series of high washboard ridges running north to south. Bordered on the west by the Sierra Nevada range and by the Rocky Mountains on the east, the land receives very little precipitation and is predominantly arid.

However, the water runoff from rains and snows which do arrive creates a number of small streams which find their ways into many rich valleys between the ridges. These streams and creeks produce rainbows and brooks. The Ruby Mountain area of Elko County is especially famous for its angling sport in small streams and high lakes.

Nevada's finest fishing is in the western part. In the north, near Reno, the Walker, Truckee, and Carson rivers flow. And there are important lakes such as Lakes Tahoe, Topaz, Pyramid, and Walker.

To the south, near Las Vegas, an important part of the Colorado River complex forms huge Lakes Mead and Mohave.

Nevada lake waters are rich and in some areas a limit of 5 rainbows has been established because the average size runs to a large 2 pounds per fish.

TYPES OF FISH

Nevada's trout family includes rainbow, the native Lahontan cutthroat, brook, brown, lake trout, and whitefish. Most prevalent is the rainbow, which averages 7 to 10 inches in small streams and 2 pounds in many lakes.

The cutthroat has achieved remarkable size in Pyramid and Walker lakes where 10 to 15 pounds is no longer startling. The world's record cutthroat, a 41-pounder, was a product of Pyramid Lake. The deep, cold waters of Mead and Mohave lakes also produce big trout.

Bass, bluegills, perch, and catfish are plentiful in lower altitude lakes, and in the hundreds of reservoirs and ponds used for water storage and farming purposes, also, in the shallows of Mead and Mohave.

Nevada has working agreements with California and Arizona affecting fishing licenses and limits in waters bordering two states. Topaz and Tahoe Lakes are on the California border and Mead and Mohave on the Arizona border. Fishermen are advised to get local information about these areas by writing to Departments of Fish and Game at any of the three states or by visiting a tackle store near the waters affected.

Licenses: Fees are $5 for residents' seasonal; $10 non-residents' seasonal; $3.50 non-residents' 5-day license. There is no charge for boys and girls 16 years and younger.

Limits: The daily limit for trout is 15 fish or 10 pounds. Other daily limits are: bass, 10 fish; catfish, 25 fish; sunfishes, 25 each type.

For additional information write Nevada Fish and Game Commission, Box 678, Reno.

New Mexico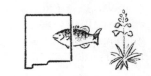

New Mexico, geographically the fifth largest state in the Union, is square in shape, measuring 400 miles wide and 400 miles long. Altitudes range from 3,000 feet to 13,000 feet above sea level.

Northern New Mexico is considered to be a part of the Rocky Mountain region and the south is part of the southwestern desert region.

The average fisherman would undoubtedly think twice or thrice before he planned a fishing trip to this land because it is often associated with heat, aridity, rattlesnakes, and mysterious nuclear experiments. But among dyed-in-the-wool anglers who know their sport, especially the fly fishermen, the state of New Mexico is a wonderful place to enjoy an early fishing vacation.

TYPES OF FISH IN NEW MEXICO

Rainbow, brown, and Yellowstone cutthroat trout are to be found in the mountain area streams and lakes of northern and central New Mexico and in the Mogollon range in the southwest. In smaller streams are rainbow and brook as well as a distant relative of the salmon family called a New Mexico cutthroat.

Largemouth black bass, bluegill, catfish, perch, walleye, and crappie are located in the lower elevation lakes and quiet reaches of slow moving rivers.

Due to its southern location, the spring runoff of water is usually over in New Mexico when the peak of the flow is just beginning further north. Consequently good fishing, especially the fly variety, can be found in May in large-sized rivers such as the Rio Grande, Gila, Chama, Rio Penasco, and their tributaries.

SEASONS, LICENSES, AND LIMITS

Seasons: U.S. Highway 66, which runs across New Mexico's middle from east to west, is an important marker for anglers to know about. South of this busy transcontinental highway the fishing season is open the year around. North of the highway the trout season continues from early May through November. This is because elevations rise abruptly north of 66 and high, forested areas are the source of excellent trout waters. There is no closed season on warmwater fish.

Licenses: License fees are $3.50 for residents' all-season; $8 for non-residents' all-season; $3 for non-residents' 5-day license. There is no charge for children 13 years and younger.

Limits: Daily limits in New Mexico are trout, 12; black bass, 12; walleye, 12; catfish, 15; crappie, 40. There is no limit on bluegill or other sunfishes.

Further information may be obtained from the Department of Game and Fish, Santa Fe.

Oregon

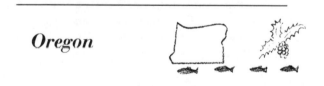

The wide variety in Oregon's climate has its effect on fishing. Rain-bearing winds at the coast sweep inland, depositing considerable moisture as far as the lofty Cascades.
Oregon is divided into two climate areas by a wall of high Cascade Mountains running north and south and reaching heights of 10,000 feet. To the west, the state is moist and densely forested and has low mountains and valleys and to the east it is a large semi-arid area.

These rains, and winter snows, create a tremendous water run-off and as a consequence the western half of the state has a huge network of lakes and streams.

Every kind of trout water and just about every type of freshwater gamefish that prospers in the West, is found here. Salmon, steelhead, and cutthroat, along with native rainbows, are the favorite tackle busters fishermen pursue. Rivers such as the Rogue, Umpqua, Deschutes, McKenzie, and others are hallowed words when anglers talk about going after these big fish.

The Wallowa Mountains in the northeast have Sierra-like conditions of less undergrowth and more warmth. Off the highway systems, this area with its thousand lakes and thousands of miles of streams, is perfect for the camper who likes to pack in.

In southeast Oregon are the Steens Mountains, a relatively little known area famed for cutthroat, rainbow, and brook trout.

In between the Wallowa and Steen areas are arid lands not often fished by tourists because they don't look promising on a map. But natives have no difficulty finding excellent sport in lakes and streams which abound; and despite the country's austere look excellent catches are made.

The central portion of Oregon is renowned as lake country.

TYPES OF FISH IN OREGON

The principle gamefish taken in coastal streams and bays include the king and silver salmons, steelhead, native rainbow, cutthroat, and striped bass. Inland are brown trout, kokanee (landlocked sockeye salmon), brooks, lake trout, and sturgeon, in addition to the coastal species. Bass, perch, sunfishes, and catfish are caught in waters throughout the state.

Due to the mildness of western Oregon's weather there is little fall-off in summer fishing. On the contrary, salmon and steelhead may be taken in coastal streams from June into October and native rainbows are always willing. Water conditions change more than the fish.

SEASONS, LICENSES, AND LIMITS

Seasons: The summer trout season opening date may vary from the middle of April to early May depending upon the locality. The season generally closes in early October.

Warmwater gamefish, including bass, catfish, perch, and crappie, may be fished for throughout the year. Late fall, winter, and early spring fishing is confined primarily to salmon and steelhead. Fishermen should consult the regulations before fishing.

Licenses: License fees are $3 for residents' all-season; $1 for resident children 12 to 15 years; No charge is made for resident children under 12 years. $10 for non-residents' all-season; $4. for non-residents' 5-day license; $5 for non-residents' 12 to 15 years all-season: $2 for non-residents' 12 to 15 years 5-day license.

Utah

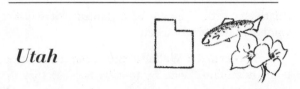

Utah is a land of towering mountains, multi-colored canyons, fertile valleys, alkali deserts, and, for the fisherman, an excellent variety of lake and stream fishing.

The greater part of the state is high plateau, averaging 6,000 feet altitude. Eleven peaks rise over two miles high and along with hundreds of less majestic but nonetheless high neighbors they provide a rich water runoff to create many excellent streams and lakes. The climate is dry and stimulating. Warm in summer and cold in winter, Utah loves to advertise its skies are clear and cloudless 300 days a year.

The Wasatch Mountains of the Rocky Mountain chain, traverse the state's middle from north to south, cutting the state in half.

To the west the desert basin, with its Great Salt Lake and Bonneville racing flats, stretches south into the southwestern desert region famous for its rainbow-colored canyons, cliffs, and natural bridges. Here the large Sevier River is the major artery.

In the north part of the state are the high Uinta Mountains, the only mountain range in the United States running from east to west.

The western slope's largest streams are the Bear, Weber, and Provo rivers. The Bear, with its tributaries, notably the Logan and Blacksmith Fork, is a renowned fishing area.

The eastern half of Utah is drained by the huge Green, San Juan, and Colorado Rivers which pour their waters through deep, eroded canyons into the Colorado basin complex.

TYPES OF FISH IN UTAH

Cool, clear streams and lakes provide fishermen with most western species favorites. However, the hatchery emphasis is on rainbow trout. Brown, brook, lake trout, and kokanee salmon are planted but not in proportion to the rainbows.

Rainbows are featured because a few years ago the state decided it could get better results if it concentrated its fish production, time, and efforts predominantly on a single gamefish species. This philosophy has helped make Utah famous for its abundance of fine rainbows.

Lakes are stocked with trout, largemouth black bass, bluegill, catfish, walleyes, and occasionally black crappie.

UTAH SEASONS, LICENSES, AND LIMITS

Seasons: The taking of fish by angling is permitted from the first Saturday in June through November 30 from 4:00 A.M. to 6:00 P.M. in all waters except as specified by the Utah Fish and Game Commission.

Licenses: License fees are $4 for residents' all-season; $10 for non-residents' all-season; $5 for non-residents' 7 consecutive day license; $2 for boys and girls 14 to 17 years. There is no charge for children under 14 years.

Limits: For trout, 10 fish or 7 lbs. of fish plus one fish are allowed daily. Other limits and information may be obtained from the Department of Fish and Game, Salt Lake City.

Washington

Washington is a state of contrasts. In the west the shores of the Pacific Ocean merge with rolling foothills, a remarkable inland bay, and craggy peaks to create heavily timbered forests, rich valleys, and farmlands.

Here the Olympic Mountains fill much of the state's large western peninsula between the ocean and Puget Sound and there are many lakes and streams to form a fisherman's paradise.

Dividing the state into east and west are the Cascade Mountains ranging up to 14,410 feet at Mt. Rainier and 12,307 feet at Mt. Adams. Peaks such as these are perpetually covered with snow. They are characterized by glaciers, windswept timberline, alpine lakes, and strong streams running down their sides.

The eastern part of Washington is considerably drier. Beginning with the eastern slopes of the Cascades this region leads into a land of rolling sage brush, broad wheatlands, rocky canyons, pastures, fruit ranches, and farms.

The Columbia River flows through here. A series of reservoirs made by giant dams slows its progress but adds to its utility. Then it swallows the large Yakima and Snake Rivers and proceeds to the sea after helping turn over one million arid acres into fruitful production.

Nearly, 8,000 named lakes are known in the state. Many are located high in the mountains but thousands of them are within 150 miles of metropolitan Seattle.

TYPES OF FISH IN WASHINGTON

Due to the many diversified waters in Washington there is a wide variety of gamefish. These include eleven kinds of trout; ten species of spiny-ray fish, the grayling, and the whitefish. The specimens which anglers visiting Washington make a special effort to catch are steelhead, salmon, and cutthroat because they run to such large size and provide so much fight.

Native gamefish include the rainbow, steelhead, cutthroat, silver, and Dolly Varden trout. Fish introduced into Washington waters include eastern brook, mackinaw, brown (Loch Leven) trout. Bass, perch, crappie, and other warmwater fishes are also present.

In western Washington many large rivers and small streams drain the melting snow and rainfall from the mountains into Puget Sound and the sea. Fish populations in these areas are often migratory. Traveling from salt to fresh water and known as anadromous fish, they are represented by the salmon, steelhead, shad, cutthroat, and rainbow. They can give anglers all the athletic action they ever hoped for.

Of an estimated 2,000 lowland lakes in Washington, approximately 80 percent have been planted with spiny-ray fish to give the bass angler an opportunity to use his favorite lures just as a trout fisherman is supplied with trout so he can cast a fly. Due to cold water temperatures these bass do not prosper as well as they do in the warmer climates of the southern states. However, though smaller in size, they are superbly conditioned to fight a big fellow's battle.

Western Washington has an equable summer climate. There is no hot sun on the western side of the Cascade Mountains or on either side of the rugged Olympic Peninsula. Therefore, summer fishing conditions are almost as good as in spring and fall. The major difference is in the fishes' desire to feed. And fish in Washington are the same as fish elsewhere; they eat more in spring after a winter of fasting and again in fall just before going into hibernation.

LICENSES AND LIMITS

Licenses: Fishing license fee for residents' all-season is $4.50. Boys and girls under 16 years, no charge. Non residents' all-season is $15. A 7-day non-resident license is $4.00

Limits: Limit for trout is 6 pounds and one fish provided the number does not exceed 12 fish. Limit for steelhead is 2 fish over 20 inches. For bass it is 20 pounds and one bass. No limit for the sunfishes.

For further information about fishing contact the Department of Game and Fish, 600 N. Capitol Way, Olympia. A detailed camping directory for the northwest region of Oregon and Washington pubished by the U.S. Forestry Service and a booklet published by the State of Washington may be obtained by writing to State of Washington Parks and Recreation Commission, 522 S. Franklin Street, Olympia. Other information may be obtained from the State of Washington Department of Commerce and Economic Development.

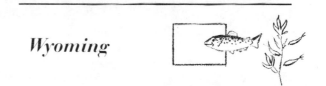

Wyoming

Wyoming's average elevation is high. Almost all of its area is more than a mile above sea level.

Straddling the Rocky Mountains, Wyoming is famous for its bright sunshine, warm summers, and clear, cold days in winter when deep snow blankets the Rockies.

The state's 20,000 miles of fishing streams and nearly 5,000 fishing lakes have made it a favorite for fishing among thousands of anglers from near and far.

Because the state is large in area and small in population with many good roads, some of the best fishing waters can be reached by automobile. Fine accommodations are often found near these waters.

Perhaps Wyoming's most renowned feature is the geologic wonder of Yellowstone National Park. Here, where scores of great geysers spout boiling water and steam higher than the trees around them, a visitor can also find many beautiful cool streams and clear lakes among dramatic mountains and lush valleys. In the Grand Teton Park, Jackson Hole, and Yellowstone complex this northwest portion of Wyoming is a tourist fisherman's paradise. He not only gets beauty, he also gets fish.

TYPES OF FISH IN WYOMING

The lakes and streams of Wyoming provide excellent fishing opportunities for trout, bass, crappie, catfish, walleye, pike, perch, grayling, and kokanee salmon.

The reason for the wide variety in such a northern locale is because the high mountain lands, and cool waters of the Rockies, are perfect for the trout family, while the plains of eastern Wyoming support the kind of lakes, ponds, and streams which warm summer suns make ideal for members of the spiny-ray family. Bass, crappies, and perch are so plentiful that no bag limit is placed on them.

WYOMING SEASONS, LICENSES

Seasons: Generally the season lasts from May 1 through October 31. There are exceptions, because many species of fish are available the year around.

Licenses: Non-resident seasonal fishing license is $12. Non-resident fishing license for 5 days is $4.